This copy of

6 Hours to 6 Figures

is presented to:

_____.___

I believe in this industry and

in your gifts and talents. I stand in agreement for

your *complete success* as a

Senior Insurance Advisor.

By:

_____

Brandon Clay Enterprises, LLC

SALES MASTERY SERIES

6 HOURS TO 6 FIGURE$

Senior Insurance Advisor Manual & Workbook

From Zero to $100k in ~~24~~ *12 -18 months!*

Brandon L. Clay

While great care has been taken to assure the accuracy of this content at time of print, it is not a substitution for reviewing, understanding and complying with all state and federal laws that govern the industry and products discussed. It is the responsibility of the licensed agent, for whom this book is intended to ensure that specific carrier guidelines are followed and that proper licensing, certification and other requirements are met.

This book is intended to be a training guide for licensed insurance agents specializing in senior insurance products and is not intended for consumer or Medicare beneficiary audiences. <u>Licensed agents must use approved materials for client interactions and this guide is not for use with consumers or Medicare beneficiaries.</u>

This publication is designed to provide accurate and authoritative information in regard to the subject matter covered. It is sold with the understanding that the publisher and author are not engaged in rendering legal, accounting, or other professional services. If legal advice or other expert assistance is required, the services of a competent professional should be sought.

Published by Createspace for Brandon Clay Enterprises, LLC
McDonough, GA
www.brandonlclay.com

Copyright © 2014 Brandon L. Clay
Createspace
ISBN-13: 978-1496076144
ISBN-10: 1496076141

Distributed by Brandon Clay Enterprises, LLC.

For ordering information or special discounts for bulk purchases, please email Brandon Clay Enterprises, LLC at bclay@brandonlclay.com

Design and composition by Brandon Clay Enterprises, LLC
Cover Design by Brandon Clay Enterprises, LLC

1st Edition

This work and *everything* I do is dedicated to my best friend and wife, Natalie. All my love and devotion!

To the millions of people, worldwide, who are pursuing greatness that may happen upon one of my works: I believe in the nobility of sales and your ability to be a top professional. My greatest desire is that something said within these pages will impact your life and set you on course to unleash all the greatness that is within you!

I wish you Money, Power, and Success!

Contents

The Power of 6 Hours to 6 Figures

Time Required: 10 Minutes

Time Remaining: 6 Hours 00 Minutes

What you will learn in this session;

4 min	Who is Brandon Clay?
5 min	6 Hours to 6 Figures
1 min	How This Training Manual Will Accelerate Your Learning Curve
10 min	Running Time

Who is Brandon Clay?

I will be brief, as I want to spend most of this time helping you become a successful Senior Insurance Advisor. Let me explain why I am uniquely qualified to assist you in that pursuit. For 18 years, I have been connected with the senior insurance industry, specifically Medicare Advantage. I won't to try dazzle you with a list of accomplishments and achievements, but rather, a quick list of companies and positions held;

- 1996 - United Healthcare – Director of Sales
- 1999 - Cigna Healthcare – Regional Director of Sales
- 2001 - Providers Direct Healthplan – Director of Sales
- 2006 - XLHealth/Care Improvement Plus – Sr. National Director of Sales

Beyond that experience, I have been in sales for 30 years, the majority of my working life. I have seen it from all angles and perspectives – from the first day newbie "thrown to the wolves", to a National Director of Sales responsible for billions of dollars in revenue. I have trained well over 35,000 sales professionals in various industries with great result. I have been classically trained by Huthwaite Institute and SPIN® training, and from the school of hard knocks of experience. *One thing the last 30 years have taught me is that each person is different and requires a different approach to help them become successful.*

As a result, I have built a philosophy and process to train people that deals with the individual *first* and the selling process secondarily. My father-in-law and sales trainer extraordinaire Leroy Shuffler says that "self-mastery must come before sales mastery". If people don't understand the nature of the opportunity in front of them, and gauge their willingness and ability to pursue it with passion and purpose, they will give a half-hearted effort and will not successful.

The last few years I have been writing sales books, particularly, business parables that demonstrate how someone new to sales can go from "struggle to success". As I toured the country and met hundreds of insurance agents, I was struck by how many of them seemed "lost" and not able to leverage the great opportunity that existed in the senior insurance market. Because my former roles only took a single product view, my only job was to explain *my company's product*.

Carriers wish they could tell you this, but most want your undivided attention...that's understandable. But the more exposure I got to the industry at large, and the commonality of the agents' struggle, I began to see a bigger picture... **one where portfolio selling rules the day.**

While there is good effort being made by agencies to train agents on portfolio selling, the vast majority of agents are still focused on one main product with a few key carriers. That makes them very vulnerable to changes in those products, compliance and regulations, and the environment in general.

Because I love this industry, I decided to use my experience, gift as a writer, and abilities as a world-class trainer to create **The 6 Hours to 6 Figures** training manual for Senior Insurance Advisors. There is a void in market place and this training manual fills it.

Before we go further...I am *not* the classic sales trainer.

Most sales books and training are targeted toward the top 20% performers who are already successful. There are many of you holding this book who are already well into the six-figure income bracket. You are earning a great living selling the products described in this manual, and in some cases, are experts in your own right. Certainly, there is something in this manual to help everyone in the industry get better and produce more business and while I truly honor and love top performers, they are *not* my primary audience.

I wrote this industry training manual for **The Newbie** *- those who are new to sales and nervous - scared of what to do...not knowing what comes next.*

I wrote it for **The Wounded Warrior** *- those lost in the process and struggling financially. Those who feel they don't have what it takes and are barely hanging on - ready to quit.*

I wrote it for **The Steady Majority** *- good performers who are working hard but are one ingredient way from reaching a higher level of success.*

I wrote it for the 80% of agents who desire to earn a great living as a Senior Insurance Advisor. Most of them are just one ingredient away from achieving it and I believe* The 6 Hours to 6 Figures *training manual is that missing ingredient.

I am uniquely qualified to write this book and have you invest time and money to read it and work the pages because of one thing...***results.***

6 Hours to 6 Figures

This manual has three main objectives;

1. To help you become a successful Senior Insurance Advisor
2. To help you become a trusted resource to the senior population – a needing and deserving audience.
3. Earn a Six Figure Income in the process – *"As you serve…you deserve"*.

Senior Insurance Advisor Portfolio Approach				
	Final Expense Foundation Product	**Medicare Supplement** (20% Of Clients Purchase)	**Medicare Advantage** (30% Of Clients Purchase)	**Hospital Indemnity** (30% Of Clients Purchase)
Total Clients	150	30	45	45
Revenue Opportunity				
	Final Expense	Medicare Supplement	Medicare Advantage	Indemnity	Total
Year 1	$57,600	$10,920	$12,765	$11,880	$93,165
Year 2	New $57,600 Renewal $4,500	New $10,920 Renewal $10,920	New $12,765 Renewal $9,585	New $11,880 Renewal $1,710	$119,880
Year 3	New $57,600 Renewal $9,000	New $10,920 Renewal $21,840	New $12,765 Renewal $19,170	New $11,880 Renewal $3,420	$146,595
Year 4	New $57,600 Renewal $13,500	New $10,920 Renewal $32,760	New $12,765 Renewal $28,755	New $11,880 Renewal $5,130	$173,310
Year 5	New $57,600 Renewal $18,000	New $10,920 Renewal $43,680	New $12,765 Renewal $38,340	New $11,880 Renewal $6,840	$200,025
Year 6	New $57,600 Renewal $22,500	New $10,920 Renewal $54,600	New $12,765 Renewal $47,925	New $11,880 Renewal $8,550	$226,740

The most successful people in this industry are earning six-figure incomes. For the purpose of this manual we will assume that you are starting at zero. The *first* finish line will be an income of $100,000, but does not stop there as the potential to go into higher six figures *is possible*. Rather than go "pie-in-the-sky", our clock will begin at $0 and build quickly to $8333 per month.

Seems impossible? Having the privilege of examining top producers, and industry insight, I know you have everything you need to be successful in this business. Doesn't matter if you don't have any marketing money, leads, or experience. I am reminded of the vintage Star Trek episode "Arena" where Capt. Kirk had to fight a cheesy reptile named the Gorn. While he was overmatched in terms of strength, he was told that everything he needed to defeat the Gorn was on the planet's surface. Coal, sulfur and other indigenous materials helped him fashion crude gunpowder and win!

It is no different for you in this industry. With your insurance license and desire, you have most of the raw materials necessary...what is needed is knowledge and courage to act on that knowledge. The **6 Hours to 6 Figures** training manual was designed to be modular, and allow you to dive in the areas of greatest need. I also know time is of the essence and you don't want to read another technical manual that you can't convert into success.

In about the time it takes to complete contracting paperwork and certification, this training manual will teach you how to sell effectively. There is nothing magical about six hours and really represents the beginning of your journey.

Another thing is required – you must do deeper. On the surface, the opportunity seems to be shrinking and the boom times over. That is only on the surface. The real answers are down below the surface, we have to go deeper.

"Smart skims the surface, but genius goes deeper." Brandon Clay

How This Training Manual Will Accelerate Your Learning Curve

There is information presented in this training manual that will frame a bigger picture of opportunity and provide additional insight to help you leverage the environment that exists today. You need good answers quick and to the point...that is what I have endeavored to do in **6 Hours to 6 Figures**...cut to the chase.

This manual will review many of the details that impact the industry but also gives you the "quick look" viewpoint.

Let me show you three pictures. How many ducks are in the first photo?

It is hard to see the ducks when the cows keep getting in the way!

To get the answer you need you have to focus and concentrate and filter out the noise from what you are really trying to see.

Today's environment is filled with chaos and the first thing we must do is eliminate the extraneous noise...

This is a much easier picture to work with. Only the vital information remains, but is still random and non-sequential.

To be successful as a Senior Insurance Advisor, we have to create order out of chaos, become organized and build a system.

It can still be easy to be overwhelmed when all the information you need is not in one place.

To work within a structured process means getting your ducks in a row! It means cutting to the chase of what is important, what is vital and what will help generate the most impact.

Throughout this manual, when you see this picture of the "Ducks in a row" it represents the simple information that will have the most impact on your success.

If you desire more information and to "go deeper" that information is available in these pages as well.

I am excited about the possibilities that exist for you in this industry and believe that the next 6 hours will change everything in your life and career...

Hit the stopwatch and let's get started!

Section 1: Understanding the Opportunity

Time Required: 30 Minutes

Time Remaining: 5 Hours 30 Minutes

	What you will learn in this session;
5 min	Is this the right career for you?
5 min	The Three Essentials of Success
20 min	Overview- The Opportunity, the Timing, the People
30 min	Running Time

Is this the right career for you?

Sales is a very rewarding profession. It combines three of the things that people want most when it comes to a career: Emancipation, Gratification and Remuneration.

Emancipation – Sales is largely an individual sport. You are free to run your own business your way. You choose which opportunities you engage in and the level of commitment you are willing to give to them.

Gratification – Sales moves the world. In the global economy, the equation of supply and demand is driven by sales. Great products would never make it into the hands consumers without sales. Solving a problem and meeting the needs of people is highly gratifying when done by a professional seller.

Remuneration – Sales professionals have the unique opportunity to control their income. In corporate environments, the most highly compensated individuals are in sales. Unlike salaried individuals, who have fixed income, people in sales truly have unlimited upside potential.

There is no doubt, that being a Senior Insurance Advisor combines these three elements in a way that can create a sustainable career. The ultimate question; *is this the right career for you?*

 In many ways, your perspective will determine the answer. Look at the following, what do you see?

Opportunityisnowhere

Some people will see "**Opportunity Is Nowhere**".

Others will see "**Opportunity Is Now Here**".

There is no right or wrong answer, and it is not an indication of optimism or pessimism. It simply defines where you are in the moment. Before we can begin learning what it takes to be successful in this industry, you have to believe that there is a chance for success. Your perspectives have to line up with what *you see.*

In this first section, we are going to take a look at the possibilities presented by the Senior Insurance Advisor industry. It is designed to give you a high level overview but we will also "go deeper" so that you can see beyond the noise and frame your own perspective. <u>At the end of this section, you will have a solid foundation of knowledge from which to make your decision to pursue this industry.</u>

The Three Essentials of Success

Everyone starts out on the road to success excited - full of enthusiasm and energy... *determined.* Along the way, they encounter people going in a different direction. They begin to wonder, *am I on the right path?*

They run into situations and circumstances that put them at odds with others...a tug of war over what they *incorrectly see* as **limited opportunity.**

Frustration sets in. The few who know what to do seem to be monopolizing opportunity, resources, and money. In an industry already wrought with high turnover and burnout, many think they have made the wrong career decision and decide *to quit.* They give up *"Three feet from gold".*

In every climate, in every environment, s*omewhere...someone* is making money!

Why not you?

How money is made always evolves. Little more than a century ago we were farmers and tradesmen bartering services...now we can exchange bitcoins as virtually earned and transferred money!

The key to putting yourself in the flow of wealth and possibilities is to understand the vital elements that have to be present. Here are the three components that make up success;

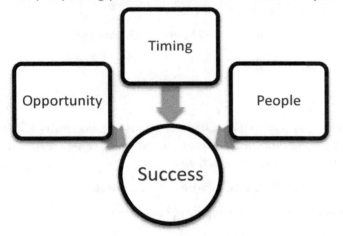

- **The *Right* Opportunity**
- **The *Right* Timing**
- **The *Right* People**

Missing any of these three ingredients will likely make success challenging or impossible. In the context of a career as a Senior Insurance Advisor, we will need to take a deeper look into these three elements so you can make the best decision for your career and business.

What does opportunity look like?

Real opportunity should not be built on chance or "the next big thing". There are some fundamental elements that define opportunity;

- What problem does it solve?
- Is it a new and emerging trend or an established industry?
- Is there an initial and growing demand?
- Are there barriers to entry so it doesn't get too crowded?
- What is the cost of entry?
- Is it right for you?

In business, timing is everything!

Windows of opportunity open and close every day. When you get in, and yes, when you get out, determines how well you do. There are some key questions to ask about timing;

- Is this a seasonal opportunity?
- Is it going to grow year after year?
- Is it a "fad" that will not sustain focused effort?
- Is the market saturated with products and/or sales people?
- Is this a ground floor opportunity and "early adopters" will have an advantage?
- Is this the right time for your business?

Are the right people in place?

Partnerships and relationships are both "ships" that can lead to Championships or sunken ships! This is the most dynamic of the three elements as human nature is sometimes unpredictable... *especially when money is involved*. A few things to consider before you build alliances;

- Is there a training and development program to cut down the learning curve?
- Will you get assistance or guidance with business development?
- Are financial models aligned so that everyone can win?
- Are the financial models aligned so that everyone has a stake in the other's success?
- Can I protect myself? As humans, *we will disappoint* each other...contracts make sure **we don't betray** each other!
- Are you ready to be committed to the partnerships?

UNDERSTANDING THE OPPORTUNITY

Having been directly involved in the industry for 17 years, I understand there have been major upheavals, drastic evolutions and barriers to success. I know many professionals who abandoned the industry when the change became *too much*. **Those changes and evolutions have actually created a new possibility for more sustainable success for the Senior Insurance Advisor who is willing to have the right perspective.**

For those new to the industry, those that are on the sidelines watching, to those that walked away, I invite you to take another look – all the ingredients are present;

- **The industry is still full of Opportunity**...*you have not been left behind!*

- **The Time is now**...look around you again, this time with a fresh perspective!

- **There are good people who sincerely desire synergistic success**...one where we form mutually beneficial partnerships *and do more than we ever thought possible!*

As with all things, you have to do what is best for your particular situation. So as you evaluate the Opportunity, Timing and People, I want you to be mindful of two Latin phrases;

Caveat Emptor – "Let the buyer beware". For the opportunities that exist, you must look at each one objectively and not blindly so that you enter into your business relationships with wisdom, and you don't look back on them with regret.

Carpe Diem – "Seize the Day". There are many sitting on the sidelines waiting for all the conditions to be perfect. That "paralysis by analysis" will keep them from leveraging the windows of opportunity that are present.

Do your due diligence, make the best determination of whether this opportunity is right for you...and take action!

Overview - The Opportunity, Timing and People

The Medicare Population is Growing Exponentially

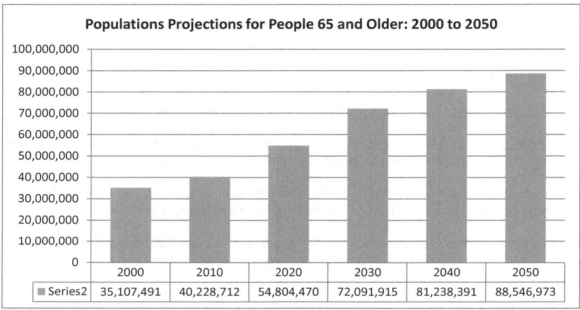

Populations Projections for People 65 and Older: 2000 to 2050

	2000	2010	2020	2030	2040	2050
Series2	35,107,491	40,228,712	54,804,470	72,091,915	81,238,391	88,546,973

NP2008_D1: Projected Population by Single Year of Age for the United States: July 1, 2000 to July 1, 2050
File: 2008 National Population Projections – Population Division, U.S Census Bureau
Release Date: August 14, 2008

- This growth rate is based on census data and reflects only those who will be turning 65 and does not include those who may become disabled and eligible for Medicare. The numbers of actual people on Medicare will be higher.

- The "10,000 people a day turning 65" advertising that is so pervasive in the media is based on these projections. That is an accurate statistic averaged out over the measured period.

- African Americans and Hispanics are growing at the fastest rate as a percentage.

There is an exponentially expanding base of potential clients who need the assistance of <u>ethical and educated</u> Senior Insurance Advisors.

The Financial Picture of People on Medicare

Components of Average Health Care Spending by Medicare Households, 2012

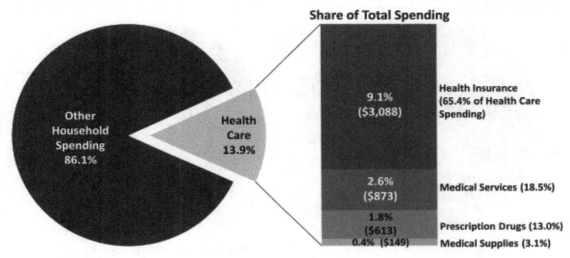

Average Total Household Spending = $33,993   Average Health Care Spending = $4,722

Note: Numbers may not sum to total due to rounding
Source: Kaiser Family Foundation analysis of the Bureau of Labor Statistics Consumer Expenditure Survey Interview and Expense Files, 2012

- For each dollar received, Medicare beneficiaries are spending $.014 on healthcare.

- There are <u>fixed costs</u> that make up the largest percentage of healthcare spending of 9.1%. These include premiums for Part B, Part D, and Medicare Supplemental to include employer plan cost.

- Healthier people are likely spending less due to lower need for episodic medical care and sicker people spend more.

- Wealthier people are likely spending less because they have supplemental coverage that limits their out-of-pocket exposure. Lower income beneficiaries are spending more as a percentage.

Distribution of Average Household Spending by Medicare and Non-Medicare Households, 2012

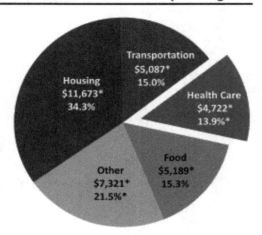

Medicare Household Spending

Transportation $5,087* 15.0%
Housing $11,673* 34.3%
Health Care $4,722* 13.9%*
Food $5,189* 15.3%
Other $7,321* 21.5%*

Average Household Spending = $33,993*

Non-Medicare Household Spending

Transportation $9,660 18.2%
Health Care $2,772 5.2%
Housing $16,976 32.0%
Food $7,890 14.9%
Other $15,702 29.6%

Average Household Spending = $53,000

Note: *Estimate statistically significantly different from non-Medicare household estimate at the 95% confidence level
Source: Kaiser Family Foundation analysis of the Bureau of Labor Statistics Consumer Expenditure Survey Interview and Expense Files, 2012

- Based on this analysis, there is a dramatic **decrease** in household income (36% drop) for Medicare households.

- There is almost a **doubling** of the dollar amount spent on health care costs (170% increase) for Medicare households...$4,722 vs. $2,772.

- Note that all other expenses by dollar amount become lower for Medicare households: Housing, transportation, food, and other.

  - Medicare Households spend $29,270 for all non-health care expenses while Non-Medicare Households spend $50,228 for all non-health care expenses

  - **That is a 42% difference in cost of "lifestyle" for Medicare households.**

Half of all Medicare beneficiaries had incomes below $23,500 per person in 2013

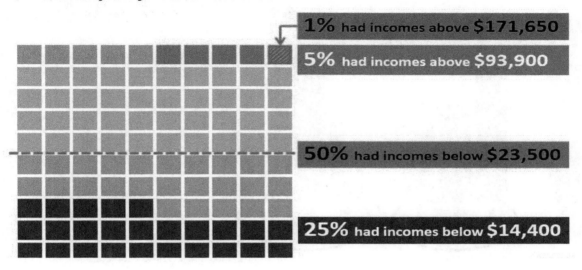

1% had incomes above **$171,650**

5% had incomes above **$93,900**

50% had incomes below **$23,500**

25% had incomes below **$14,400**

Half of all Medicare beneficiaries had savings below $61,400 per person in 2013

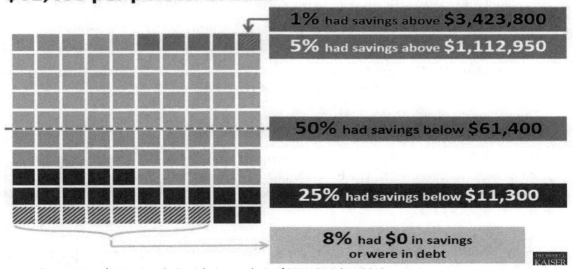

1% had savings above **$3,423,800**

5% had savings above **$1,112,950**

50% had savings below **$61,400**

25% had savings below **$11,300**

8% had **$0** in savings or were in debt

Source: Urban Institute/Kaiser Family Foundation analysis of DYNASIM data 2013.

Median per capita income among Medicare beneficiaries varies by beneficiary characteristics in 2013

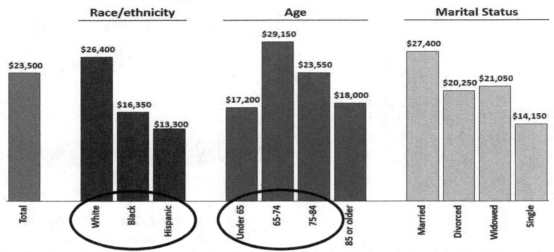

Note: Total household income for couples is split equally between husbands and wives to estimate income for married beneficiaries

Source: Urban Institute / Kaiser Family Foundation analysis, 2013

- Based on these charts, at least 50% of Medicare households struggle to make ends meet.

- Depending on number of people in the household, many are below the Federal Poverty Limits (FPL) which may qualify them for various levels of federal and state assistance.

- The wealthiest 5% that have Modified Adjusted Gross Incomes (MOGI) of $85,000 (single) and $170,000 (couple) pay more for Part B and Part D coverage.

- The variability of healthcare costs makes a large segment of the population vulnerable to paying for that care when costs are not predictable or fixed.

- Due to limited savings, many Medicare households are one health care episode away from major financial challenges. **The financial picture is even more challenging for the disabled (under 65) on Medicare, African American and Hispanics, and for those aged 75 and older.**

 The financial outlook for the Medicare population necessitates the need for financial alternatives that can provide predictability of cost and quality healthcare options.

The Health Care Options Are Many

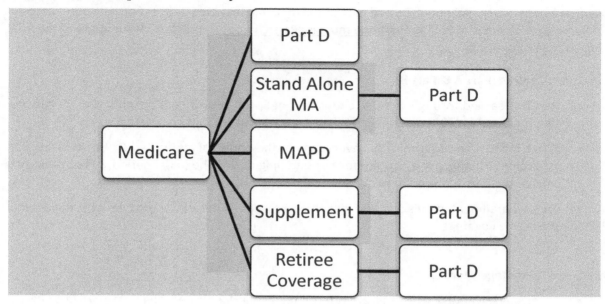

Type of Coverage	Options	Costs
Medicare	Part A & Part B	Premiums (Part B & Plan), deductibles, coinsurance, day/dollar limits, coverage gaps (Part D), benefit periods, Out of Network, etc.
Medicare Advantage	HMO, POS. PPO, RPPO, LPPO, PFFS	
Medicare Supplements	A,B,C,D,F*,G,K,L,M,N *Also high deductible	
Part D	Varies	
Duals	QI, QDWI, FDBE, SLMB, SLMB+, QMB, QMB+	
Retiree Coverage	Offered and subsidized by employer	Vary based on options available - May require a Part D plan

Within each element of the graphic and chart above, there are a myriad of choices facing the Medicare beneficiary. Additionally, and part of the dynamic that creates great opportunity for the Senior Insurance Advisor, **is that everyone must make a choice.** Here is a brief summary of the broad range of options;

Medicare Choices (Part A & Part B)

- Part A is earned through working and is part of Social Security deduction (FICA). It can also be purchased for a premium if enough quarter hours were not completed.

- Three months before turning 65, everyone has the option of taking Part B. While taking Part B is voluntary, **there is a penalty** for not enrolling during the initial period. **That penalty is 10% of the Part B premium per year.**

- These enrollment provisions and penalties are not in effect for people who have other creditable coverage.

Medicare Advantage (Part C)

- Medicare Advantage programs are offered under the Medicare program umbrella as Part C. They are private health plans that cover everything Original Medicare covers along with additional benefits. Many also cover Part D prescription drug coverage (MA-PD).

- There may be a monthly plan premium, but many are zero premium plans. They require Part A and Part B to join.

- The different types of Medicare advantage plans have mainly to do with how a member accesses the physicians, hospitals and medical services. These range from network driven HMOs to open access RPPOs.

- With the exception of End Stage Renal Disease (ESRD), and Chronic Illness Special Needs Plans (C-SNP), there is no underwriting. There are periods of open enrollment where all may join but certain limitations to when and if people may change plans.

Medicare Supplements

- Commonly referred to as Medigap policies. They are sold by private health insurance companies as supplemental insurance to Medicare Part A and B.

- They supplement Original Medicare and help pay for "gaps" in coverage like deductibles, coinsurance and copayments. Some cover things Medicare doesn't.

- Medicare supplements are standardized with a few variations based on the state. The 11 options are; Plans A, B, C, D, F, G, K, L, M, and N - Plan F has a high-deductible option. The insurance companies don't have to sell all plans.

- Due to standardization, only the premiums will vary by company.

- For beneficiaries, there are guaranteed issue periods and trial rights that create opportunities to change from one company or plan to another. Outside of these provisions, companies can underwrite coverage.

Prescription Drug Program (Part D)

- Part D prescription drug coverage is offered through Medicare approved private insurance companies. It could be a standalone plan (PDP) or included in a Medicare Advantage plan (MA-PD).

- There is a minimally acceptable standard, set by the government, which all plans must maintain.

- Part D is voluntary. If a Medicare beneficiary does not elect a Part D program during the initial enrollment period, **they pay a penalty of 1% per month for each month they became eligible but did not enroll.**

- These enrollment provisions and penalties are not in effect for people who have other creditable coverage.

- Low Income Subsidy (LIS) is available for some Part D participants based on income levels. They receive support ranging from lower premiums, lower cost-sharing and assistance through the coverage gap, commonly referred to as the "doughnut hole".

- The Affordable Care Act of 2010 (ACA/Obamacare) has made provisions to eliminate the doughnut hole through discounts and systematic closure of the coverage gap by 2020.

Dual Eligibles (Medicare and Medicaid)

- Medicare beneficiaries that fall within certain ranges of the Federal Poverty Limits (FPL) are eligible for additional benefits at a state level – Medicaid.

- While the levels vary, most of these beneficiaries pay very little for healthcare as the deductibles and cost-sharing for Part A and Part B are paid for by Medicaid.

- The majority also do not pay the Part B premium.

- Most dual eligibles also receive LIS and do not pay a Part D premium and receive all the previously described benefits of that subsidy.

- Even with the rich benefits they receive, many Dual Eligibles are opting for Medicare Advantage plans specifically designed for them known as Dual Special Needs Plans (D-SNP).

Retiree Coverage

- A segment of the Medicare population has coverage through their employer. They may have a spouse that is still working and covering them under their insurance plan.

- If retired, Medicare is the primary and their retiree coverage is secondary or supplemental.

- For most retiree plans, if the beneficiary opts out of it, they cannot opt back into the coverage in the future.

- There is also a host of governmental and military based coverage, some of which have no coordination of benefits, such as VA, which would allow for flexibility. Others are fully self-contained and additional options may be detrimental, such as Tricare.

- There are many kinds of coverage. The best way to determine the options that may be available would be to contact the Plan Administrator of the employer providing the coverage.

The sheer number of options and the complexity of each is daunting for someone moving into Medicare and retirement.

The vast majority of eligibles enroll in Medicare Part A, Part B and Part D.

Due to gaps in coverage they have to select the most comprehensive coverage that <u>they can afford</u>.

This creates a need for specific insurance, financial and healthcare solutions and the services of a professional Senior Insurance Advisor to help them navigate the complex choices.

The Medicare Advantage Environmental Overview

The High Cost of Medicare Is Growing

Medicare Benefit Payments By Type of Service, 2012

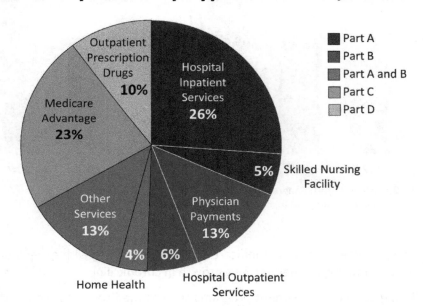

Total Benefit Payments = $536 billion

NOTE: Excludes administrative expenses and is net of recoveries. *Includes hospice, durable medical equipment, Part B drugs, outpatient dialysis, ambulance, lab services, and other services.
SOURCE: Kaiser Family Foundation as derived from Congressional Budget Office (CBO) Medicare Baseline, February 2013.

- Original Medicare is a Fee – For – Service model and pays only when someone seeks services, which leads to an unpredictability and variability of cost.

- The 23% paid to Medicare Advantage private insurance companies is a <u>fixed cost</u> and in most cases, the risk is passed to the insurer.

- Medicare is one of the largest line items on the federal budget and is a federally mandated expense.

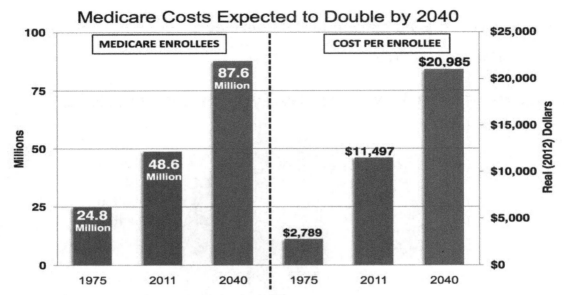

SOURCE: 2012 Trustees Report, Congressional Budget Office.
Produced by Veronique De Rugy, Marcatus Center at George Mason University

- The projected growth in Medicare beneficiaries, along with expectations of longer life, while at the same time experiencing a growth in chronic illness all indicates higher expenditures.

- Rising costs of entitlement programs such as Medicare and Medicaid and the fact that they are federally mandatory budget items means that a solution has to be found for lowering cost or raising revenue (taxes).

- As the Affordable Care Act of 2010 is implemented, there will be other factors such as the expansion of Medicaid, systematic closure of the coverage gap for Part D, creation of Accountable Care Organizations (ACO's), and reimbursement methodology to doctors and Medicare Advantage companies, which will have an impact on the financial outlook.

- The outcome of proposed private health insurer rate reductions (Medicare Advantage) and the "Doctor Fix" (Medicare payments to providers) create uncertainty about the environment as the budget impasse continues politically.

Politics will always have an impact on the future of Medicare and corresponding programs, largely in the form of reimbursement and payments.

The complexity of the rising population and costs, mandate that some form of privatization will exist due to transference of risk from the government to the insurer.

The landscape will change but the educated Senior Insurance Advisor will be able to stay abreast, govern their businesses accordingly, and help their clients navigate the evolving choices!

Medicare Advantage Enrollment

Total Medicare Private Health Plan Enrollment, 1999-2013

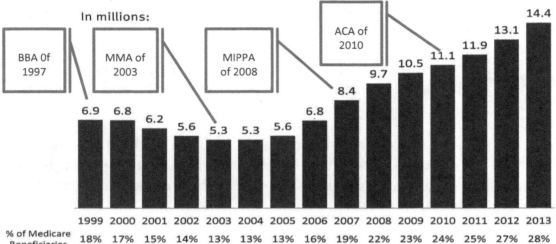

NOTE: Includes, MSAs, cost plans, demonstration plans, and Special Needs Plans as well as other Medicare Advantage plans.
SOURCE: MPR/Kaiser Family Foundation analysis of CMS Medicare Advantage enrollment files, 2008 – 2013, and MPR, "Tracking Medicare Health and Prescription Drug Plans Monthly Report," 2001-2007; enrollment numbers from March of the respective year, with the exception of 2006, which is from April

Share of Medicare Beneficiaries Enrolled in Medicare Advantage Plans, by State, 2013

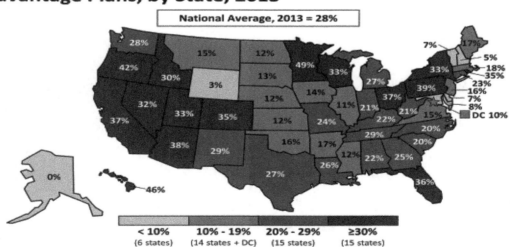

NOTE: Includes MSAs, cost plans and demonstrations. Includes Special Needs Plans as well as other Medicare Advantage Plans as well as other Medicare Advantage plans.
SOURCE: MPR/Kaiser Family Foundation analysis of CMS State/County Market Penetration Files, 2013

- 1999 to 2003 represents the only decline in enrollment and was largely driven by the Balanced Budget Act of 1997 (BBA) when reimbursements were lowered to private health companies. In the absence of risk adjusted payments many insurers left the market.

- The Medicare Modernization Act of 2003 greatly expanded the Medicare program with risk adjusted payments, Part D pharmacy program, Chronic Illness Special Needs Plans (C-SNPs), Dual Special Needs Plans (D-SNPs) and **allowing brokers to market the products**.

- Growth as a number and percentage of eligibles has increased each year since 2004 even with the impact of Medicare Improvements for Patients and Providers Act of 2008 (MIPPA) and The Affordable Care Act of 2010 (ACA/Obamacare).

- Nationally, 28% (almost 1 in 3) people are selecting Medicare Advantage and 20% of the Dual Eligibles (Medicare and Medicaid) are joining some form of Managed Care plan.

- Regions of the country with lower penetration/enrollment rates, are largely due to lack of access. Medicare Advantage plans such as Private Fee for Service Plans (PFFS) and Regional Preferred Provider Organizations (RPPOs) were instituted to give greater access to rural areas.

- Some areas with higher enrollment have mature markets, concentration of seniors (CA, AZ, FL, etc.) and attractive benefits due to historically higher reimbursement.

Number of Medicare Plans and Distribution by Carrier

Number of Medicare Advantage Plans Available, by Plan Availability Status, 2013 and 2014

Each ▦ is equivalent to about 6 plans

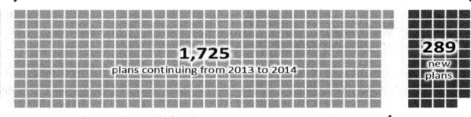

2,014 plans available in 2014

349 discontinued plans

1,725 plans continuing from 2013 to 2014

289 new plans

2,074 plans available in 2013

NOTE: Excludes SNPs, employer-sponsored (i.e., group) plans, demonstrations, HCPPs, PACE plans, and plans for special populations (e.g., Mennonites).

SOURCE: MPR/Kaiser Family Foundation analysis of CMS's Landscape Files for 2013 – 2014.

Medicare Advantage Enrollment, by Firm or Affiliate, 2013

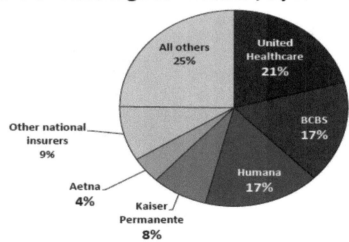

All others 25%

United Healthcare 21%

BCBS 17%

Humana 17%

Kaiser Permanente 8%

Aetna 4%

Other national insurers 9%

Total Medicare Advantage Enrollment, 2013 = 14.4 Million

NOTE: Other included firms with less than 3% of total enrollment. BCBS are BlueCross BlueShield affiliates and includes Wellpoint BCBS plans that comprise 4% of all enrollment (558,833 enrollees) In Medicare Advantage plans; approximately 47,000 beneficiaries are enrolled in other Wellpoint plans. Other national insurers includes 1,228,443 enrollees across the following firms: Cigna (438,252), Coventry (305,584), Wellcare (252,563), Universal American (127,340), Munich Holding Corporation (57,697), and Wellpoint non-BCBS plans (47,007). **Percentages may not sum to 100% due to rounding.**
SOURCE: MPR/Kaiser Family Foundation analysis of CMS Enrollment files, 2013.

- While there is a measure of consolidation and termination of plans for various reasons that impact the number of plans available, the Medicare Advantage platforms of products is generally expanding.

- For the "Big Three"; United Healthcare, Humana and the Blue Cross Blue Shield companies, Medicare Advantage and related products represent a large and growing component of their businesses.

- Major carriers such as CIGNA, Aetna, Coventry, WellCare and others are using consolidation, mergers and geographic product expansion to increase their market share and to leverage their current employer membership base which will become Medicare eligible over the next few decades.

- Regional carriers, Physician Hospital Organizations (PHO) and local healthcare delivery systems will begin to enter the arena as expanded choice, such as Accountable Care Organizations (ACO) and other programs give them the ability to enter the Medicare Advantage marketplace.

As choice and options have increased, more people have opted to join Medicare Advantage.

Regardless of political environment and executive leadership, the evolving dynamics have not slowed enrollment…it has increased and provides the Senior Insurance Advisor with opportunity to serve the Medicare/Medicaid population.

Understanding the options and the "Best Fit" program is the key to helping the beneficiary – who may be making a financially driven decision but do not want to sacrifice access to quality healthcare.

Complex Equation Made Simple

What is the future outlook for Medicare Advantage?

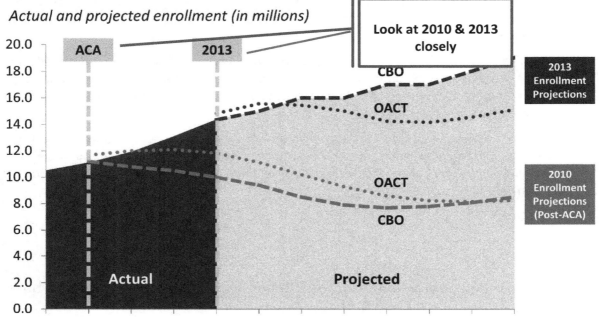

Actual and projected enrollment (in millions)

Note: CBO is Congressional Budget Office: OACT is CMS Office of the Actuary.

Source: MPR/Kaiser Family Foundation analysis of CMS Medicare Advantage enrollment files 2009-2013. CBO, "Medicare Baseline," August 2010 and May 2013. Report of the Medicare Board of Trustees, 2010 and 2013

- In 2010, both the Congressional Budget Office (CBO) and CMS office of the Actuary (OACT) predicted that Medicare Advantage Enrollment would **decrease**. *Both of these projections should be politically "agnostic" and neutral to party.*

- Despite these projections, "actual" Medicare Advantage enrollment increased, creating a substantial gap between what was expected and what occurred.

- In 2013, both agencies re-forecast their projections and both show a straight-line increase in enrollment for two additional years.

- After two years, the OACT shows a precipitous drop in 2016 (post-election?) while the CBO (which measures budget) sees a "some up...some down" yearly trend but indicates overall that enrollment will continue to grow, with membership approaching 19 million (from current 2013 levels of 14.4 million) by 2020.

While a discussion on Medicare Advantage has to include the Politics and the Products, the most important thing to remember is the <u>Policyholders</u> – *the beneficiaries*.

According to all we have reviewed, the question to ask is not what **Democrats** think, or what **Republicans** think...

Sit down at the kitchen table and ask a Medicare beneficiary what they think and what do they need?

The last chart tells the story...<u>they are joining MA plans in record numbers despite projections.</u>

While it is difficult to build a straight line of opportunity when there are so many complex moving pieces, ultimately, <u>we live in a supply and demand economy</u>. Which means if there are people that need something, *someone will create it.*

The private insurance carriers have much at stake as well. They will react to regulatory actions and reimbursement fluctuations with evolving products...

<u>Options will remain in the marketplace.</u>

While it is true that the environment is ever-evolving, a professional Senior Insurance Advisor can stay abreast of the changes and continue a path of service to their clients and career success.

The Medicare Supplement Environmental Overview

The Politics of Medigap

As we have just reviewed the Medicare Advantage environment, we now need to turn our attention to another viable option – Medicare Supplements, commonly referred to as Medigap. Because of the amount of attention given to Medicare Advantage from a compliance and regulatory standpoint, Medigap plans are not as broadly understood. Let's begin this environmental overview by recalling the fact that these plans have also undergone legislative review and changes that impact the product. Most notably, the Omnibus Budget Reconciliation Act of 1990 (OBRA) which brought about the standardization of plans that we see today.

Since Medigap policies coordinate with Fee for Service Original Medicare, the primary insurer is Medicare. Purchasers of Medigap policies are looking to cover themselves against the "gaps". In exchange for this gap coverage, policyholders pay a monthly premium.

Specifically for plans "C" and plan "F", the beneficiary has "first dollar coverage" which removes any barrier to accessing care from the individuals cost perspective. There are studies that indicate Medigap owners access considerably more care than those without the coverage since there is no financial impact or burden, particularly for those in first dollar coverage plans.

There is current discussion about making changes to Medigap policies. The focus is on attempting to curb utilization through higher cost-sharing models in an attempt to mitigate the budget impact of the growing Medicare population, and the corresponding increase in healthcare cost.

This section will deal environmentally with how the <u>consumer</u> behaves in the current marketplace.

Why the Senior Insurance Advisor <u>must</u> add Medicare Supplemental to their portfolio, stay abreast of the changes, and serve their clients with the <u>best option</u> to meet their needs.

Medigap is a popular option

Nearly one in four Medicare beneficiaries had a Medigap policy as a supplemental source of coverage in 2010

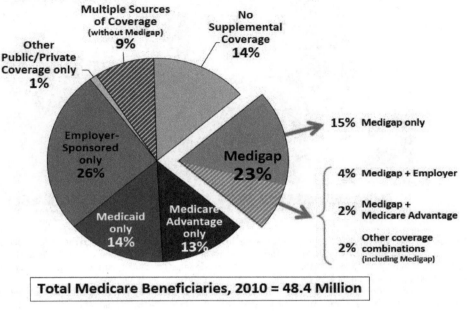

Total Medicare Beneficiaries, 2010 = 48.4 Million

SOURCE: Kaiser Family Foundation analysis of the CMS Medicare Current Beneficiary Survey Cost and Use File, 2010.

- Despite the potential of annually rising premiums, Medigap policies are still a popular option.

- People are opting for the predictability of premiums against the variable and potentially unlimited cost of Original Medicare gaps.

- Medicare Advantage plans have CMS mandated Stop-Loss provisions (Out-of Pocket Maximums), that typically exceed the annual premium of a Medigap policy and a many beneficiaries don't want that risk.

- There are no network restrictions (HMO/gatekeeper) and Medigap policyholders have open access, as long as providers accept Medicare.

Medigap and Medicare Advantage Marketplace Parity

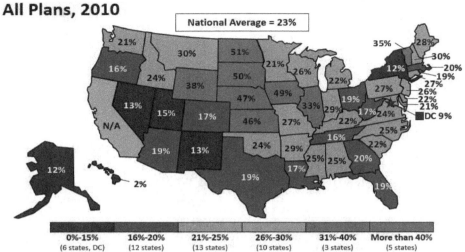

Percent of Medicare Beneficiaries with Medigap by State, All Plans, 2010

National Average = 23%

0%-15%	16%-20%	21%-25%	26%-30%	31%-40%	More than 40%
(6 states, DC)	(12 states)	(13 states)	(10 states)	(3 states)	(5 states)

NOTE: Analysis excludes California, as the majority of health insurers do not report their data to the NAIC. Analysis includes standardized plans A-N, policies existing prior to federal standardization, plans in Massachusetts, Minnesota, and Wisconsin that are not part of the federal standardization program, and plans that identified as Medicare Select; excludes plans where number of covered lives was less than 20. Number of Medigap policyholders as of December 31, 2010, as reported in the NAIC data.

SOURCE: K. Desmond, T. Rice, and Kaiser Family Foundation analysis of 2010 National Association of Insurance Commissioners (NAIC) Medicare Supplement data. Kaiser Family foundation and Mathematica Policy Research analysis of CMS State/County Market Penetration Files.

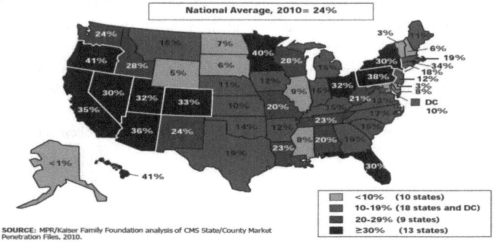

Share of Medicare Beneficiaries Enrolled in Medicare Advantage Plans, by State, 2010

National Average, 2010= 24%

<10%	(10 states)
10-19%	(18 states and DC)
20-29%	(9 states)
≥30%	(13 states)

SOURCE: MPR/Kaiser Family Foundation analysis of CMS State/County Market Penetration Files, 2010.

SOURCE: MPR/Kaiser Family Foundation analysis of CMS State/County Market Penetration Files, 2010

The Economics of Medigap

Distribution of Income of Medicare Beneficiaries, by Source of Supplemental Coverage, 2010

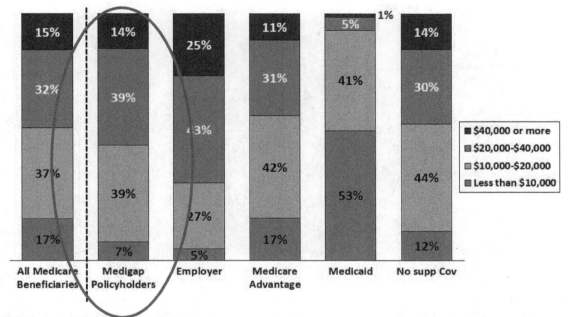

NOTE: Numbers do not sum due to rounding.
SOURCE: Kaiser Family Foundation analysis of the CMS Medicare Current Beneficiary Survey Cost and Use File, 2010.

- This chart describes the income level of the people purchasing Medigap policies. 85% have incomes below $40,000 and 46% have incomes below 20,000.

- This chart indicates that affordability is not the key driver in consumer decision. Access to care and predictable cost with limited exposure is driving choice.

- There are several other factors governing affordability, but for the Senior Insurance Advisor, the demand for this product require it be part of their portfolio.

First dollar coverage plans are most popular

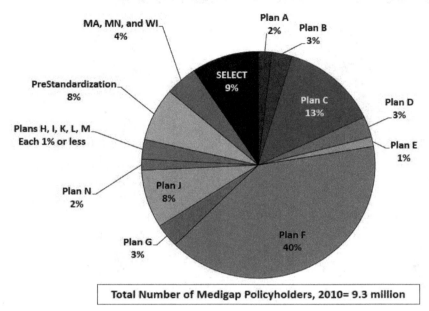

Share of Medigap Policyholders by All Plan Types, 2010

Total Number of Medigap Policyholders, 2010= 9.3 million

NOTE: Analysis excludes California, as the majority of health insurers do not report their data to the NAIC. Analysis includes standardized plans A-N, policies existing prior to federal standardization (Pre-Standardization), and plans in Massachusetts, Minnesota, and Wisconsin that are not part of the federal standardization program; includes plans that identified as Medicare Select; excludes plans where number of covered lives was less than 20. Number of Medigap policyholders as of December 31, 2010, as reported in the NAIC data.
SOURCE: K. Desmond, T. Rice, and Kaiser Family Foundation analysis of 2010 National Association of Insurance Commissioners (NAIC) Medicare Supplement data.

- Current standardization provides for up to 11 plan options (Plan F has high deductible option).

- The most purchased plans are Plan C and Plan F.

- Those two plans have "first dollar coverage" and pay all gaps associated with Original Medicare.

- Note: A Part D pharmacy plan, or other creditable coverage is required or penalties may be incurred.

Medigap policies will continue to be a *strong choice* for a segment of the Medicare population.

Affordability is a consideration but not the primary driver of choice.

The geographic availability of zero premium Medicare Advantage plans has slowed demand for Medigap policies generally but is now being sold at a 1:1 ratio...

For every Medicare Advantage enrollment, someone is selecting Medigap.

Plan C and Plan F, as first dollar coverage plans, are the most popular coverage options and should be the focus of the Senior Insurance Advisor.

Many private insurance carriers offer <u>both</u> Medicare Advantage and Medigap policies to leverage the growing opportunity and to be prepared to adjust to any environmental changes... *political or otherwise.*

The educated Senior Insurance Advisor should see Medicare Advantage and Medicare Supplemental in the same light – <u>offering both based on the best fit option for their clients.</u>

Hospital Indemnity Environmental Overview

Hospital indemnity has recently become part of the conversation due to provisions of the Affordable Care Act of 2010 (ACA/Obamacare). The heart of review is to ensure that this type of policy is not being used as a substitute for major medical coverage along with other items outlined in the law. There is a different treatment of group medical plans and individual plans...*such as those purchased to help defray the costs of Medicare products.*

Here is the latest FAQ response on Hospital Indemnity from Centers for Medicare & Medicaid Services (CMS) issued on **January 9, 2014 -** (Bold and underlined text are inserted to indicate specific references to individual indemnity products that would be applicable to Medicare beneficiaries.)

Affordable Care Act Implementation FAQs (Set 18)

Fixed Indemnity Insurance

Fixed indemnity insurance provided under a group health plan meeting the conditions outlined in the Departments' regulations[14] is an excepted benefit under PHS Act section 2791(c)(3)(B), ERISA section 733(c)(3)(B), and Code section 9832(c)(3)(B). As such, it is generally exempt from the health coverage requirements of title XXVII of the PHS Act, part 7 of ERISA, and chapter 100 of the Code. The Departments have noticed a significant increase in the number of health insurance policies labeled as fixed indemnity insurance.

A previous FAQ provided guidance reiterating that, in order for a fixed indemnity policy to be considered an excepted benefit, it must pay on a per-period basis, and that a fixed indemnity policy that pays on a per-service basis does not meet the conditions for excepted benefits.[15]

Q11: If insurance labeled as fixed indemnity insurance provides benefits other than on a per-period basis, may the insurance nonetheless qualify as excepted benefits?

Yes. With respect to group health insurance coverage that does not meet the definition of fixed indemnity excepted benefits, coverage that supplements other group health plan coverage may, nonetheless, qualify as supplemental excepted benefits under sections 2722(c)(3) and 2791(c)(4) of the PHS Act, sections 732(c)(3) and 733(c)(4) of ERISA, and sections 9831(c)(3) and 9832(c)(4) of the Code. See 26 CFR 54.9831-1(c)(5); 29 CFR 2590.732(c)(5); 45 CFR 146.145(c)(5); the Department of Labor's Employee Benefits Security Administration's Field Assistance Bulletin No. 2007-04 (available at http://www.dol.gov/ebsa/pdf/fab2007-4.pdf); HHS Centers for Medicare & Medicaid Services Insurance Standards Bulletin 08-01 (available at http://www.cms.gov/CCIIO/Resources/Files/Downloads/hipaa_08_01_508.pdf) ; and Internal Revenue Service Notice 2008-23 (available at http://www.irs.gov/irb/2008-07_IRB/ar09.html).

Furthermore, HHS intends to propose amendments to 45 CFR 148.220(b)(3) **that would allow fixed indemnity coverage sold in the individual health insurance market to be considered to be an excepted benefit if it meets the following conditions:**

1. It is sold only to individuals who have other health coverage that is minimum essential coverage within the meaning of section 5000A(f) of the Code;

2. There is no coordination between the provision of benefits and an exclusion of benefits under any other health coverage;

3. The benefits are paid in a fixed dollar amount regardless of the amount of expenses incurred and without regard to the amount of benefits provided with respect to an event or service under any other health coverage; and

4. A notice is displayed prominently in the plan materials informing policyholders that the coverage does not meet the definition of minimum essential coverage and will not satisfy the individual responsibility requirements of section 5000A of the Code.

If these proposed revisions are implemented, fixed indemnity insurance in the individual market would no longer have to pay benefits solely on a per-period basis to qualify as an excepted benefit. Until HHS finalizes this rulemaking related to these proposed amendments, **HHS will treat fixed indemnity coverage in the individual market as excepted benefits for enforcement purposes if it meets the conditions above in States where HHS has direct enforcement authority**. For States with primary enforcement authority, HHS encourages those States to also treat this coverage as an excepted benefit and will not consider that a State is not substantially enforcing the individual market requirements merely because it does so.

> While it should not be deemed as formal guidance, Hospital Indemnity plans sold to Medicare beneficiaries would meet the test for excepted benefits.
>
> Hospital copays are typically the single largest exposure of a Medicare Advantage plan. *One hospital stay can negate the cost savings of a zero-premium plan.*
>
> Other cost-sharing exposures create the need for Hospital Indemnity plans and the educated Senior Insurance Advisor should have them in their portfolio.

Life Insurance Environmental Overview

Of all the products we will review, life insurance has remained largely unchanged and is not directly impacted by current governmental or regulatory actions beyond those already established for the industry. It is also a product of relative simplicity as compared to Medicare products, typically driven by face amount and premium.

Part of the rationale of allowing brokers to sell Medicare Advantage and Part D through the Medicare Modernization act of 2003, was due to the stability/demand of life insurance and the large "kitchen table" sales force that distributed the product. The fact that life insurance must be sold 48 hours outside of the Medicare product arena is testament to that philosophy of distribution. Final Expense and other senior related products go hand in hand with consumer need and the sales continuum.

While life insurance, specifically Final Expense, is a recognized necessity it does not always come with the immediacy of need that health insurance does. Life insurance is a voluntary purchase, and while mortality is on the minds of an aging population, the decision to purchase it is often delayed. When the need does present itself, many are concerned about their health status and affordability. Final Expense insurance helps bridge the gap between insurability and affordability.

Here are a few statistics from LIMRA outlining the current insurance environment (*All facts are from several of LIMRA's life insurance consumer studies*);

- Thirty percent of U.S. households have no life insurance at all; only 44 percent have individual life insurance.

- When surveyed on financial issues, "money for a comfortable retirement" was the top pick of 67 percent of consumers. By contrast, concerns that life insurance coverage traditionally addresses (such as premature death, funeral expenses and leaving an inheritance) registered as a top priority for less than 40 percent of consumers surveyed.

- Consumers who believe they need life insurance, 86 percent haven't bought it because they think it is too expensive.

- When life insurance is suggested (either by a financial professional or through advertising), 37 percent of people surveyed shopped for life insurance.

- Among households saying they are likely to buy life insurance in the next 12 months, 35 percent say the reason they have not yet bought more life insurance is because no one has approached them about it.

"Most insurance is still purchased face to face from a sales person at the kitchen table, and with fewer agents knocking on doors, there's less of it getting bought. " Byron Udell, Chief Executive of AccuQuote.

Final expense life insurance is the perfect lead-in product for the ethical and educated Senior Insurance Advisor. Marketing activities, beyond the Do Not Call Registry (DNC), and other general marketing practices, are not governed or regulated. More traditional prospecting methods such as canvassing and telemarketing are acceptable.

The resulting Existing Business Relationship (EBR) through the sale of final expense insurance allows for a fluid and compliant way to transition to other lines of business.

Everyone is a potential client for life insurance and it creates an expanding market of opportunity. There are a great deal of people, particularly in the senior market, who are either underinsured or uninsured.

The financial hardship of death is even more impactful to the senior population, who have limited savings and earning potential for the survivor.

Generally, life insurance is still predominantly sold in a face-to-face "kitchen table" environment. The majority of those interactions are generated from the marketing activities of the agents or the companies.

With a range of products designed to bridge the gap between insurability and affordability, Final Expense should be the foundational product for every Senior Insurance Advisor.

Section One Summary

Section One Summary

- The number of Medicare beneficiaries is expanding quickly and will reach unprecedented levels over the next several decades.

- The financial impact to the beneficiary and the government are increasing exponentially.

- The available programs are constantly evolving, creating new and emerging opportunity.

- In the transition to retirement and Medicare, everyone must make a choice and select the best options.

- The choices are numerous, creating confusion in the marketplace.

- People want the most comprehensive coverage they can afford leveraging the full range of healthcare and insurance options.

- People are underinsured for Life Insurance at a time they are most vulnerable to insurability and affordability.

- Medicare products (Advantage and Supplemental) enrollment is projected to continue to grow in close to a 1:1 ratio.

- People need a trusted advisor to help them navigate the complex choices.

- The ethical and educated Senior Insurance Advisor can build a high six-figure income in an environment of service to a needing and deserving population… *"As you serve…you deserve"*

What does it all mean?

Opportunity Is Now Here!

End of Section One

SECTION NOTES

_____

_____

_____

_____

_____

_____

_____

_____

_____

_____

_____

_____

_____

_____

_____

_____

_____

_____

SECTION NOTES

Section 2: The Portfolio of Products

Time Required: 1 Hour 00 Minutes

Time Remaining: 4 Hours 30 minutes

What you will learn in this session;

10 min	The Power of the Portfolio Approach
10 min	The Product Overviews
25 min	Understanding the Options
15 min	The Power of Hospital Indemnity
90 min	Running Time

The Power of the Portfolio Approach

The Basic Products

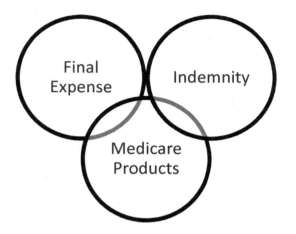

Here are the three core basic products we will need to service our clients and build a sustainable career as a Senior Insurance Advisor. They include Final Expense, Medicare products of Medicare Advantage and Medicare Supplemental, and finally Hospital indemnity.

Note: While not included as a specific product you will also need access to Part D pharmacy plans. In many respects, Part D pharmacy plans are much like Medigap plans because their core design is mandated by federal standards. The differences will be premium, co-pay levels and formulary. They can usually be contracted with the same companies with which you do Medicare Advantage.

While there are other products that can help meet the needs of the senior population, these are the foundation. Products, such as critical illness plans, provide coverage in the event of diseases like cancer. There is long-term care to help provide assistance in the event someone needs a nursing home. Annuities and other financial products are also part of the complete financial strategy for many seniors.

One of the challenges of a beginning Senior Insurance Advisor is trying to be "all things to all people". As your business progresses and your client base grows, these and other products would be natural additions to your portfolio.

As you will see in the remainder of this section, these three products will set the stage for you becoming a trusted advisor, build a structured business that is scalable, and create a firm foundation on which you can add and build.

 **Final Expense, Medicare Products and Hospital Indemnity are the foundation of the Senior Insurance Advisor portfolio.**

Advantages of Portfolio Selling

The logic of combining these three products will become evident as we review them. From the perspective of the beneficiary which would you rather deal with?

Three different agents coming to show you one product each, or one agent who is qualified to lead and guide to the best fit solution?

Make no mistake, if you are selling Final Expense insurance only today, according to statistics, 28% of your clients are buying Medicare Advantage and 20% are buying Medicare Supplemental. That works in reverse if you are selling Medicare Advantage and not the others. Even the carriers are marketing the additional products to the clients you bring to them with the "one product mentality". The real question as it relates to lost opportunity;

Is someone else finishing the work you started?

Beyond the benefit to the consumer to work with *one professional*, to have one person know the core of their situation and to have that person advise them on an annual review basis, there are many benefits to you the trusted Senior Insurance Advisor:

It allows you to work smarter not harder. The number one challenge facing most agents is lead generation. In an upcoming section when we review commission, each individual product does provide on its own, a six-figure opportunity. But in order to realize that income possibility, you need a steady stream of *new clients* – which takes time, energy and money. The portfolio approach leverages your current client base and maximizes it allowing you to make more money with fewer clients.

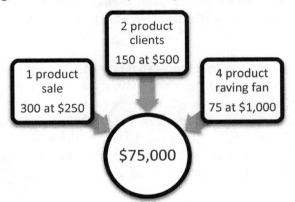

More products sold to a client means higher persistency. As the diagram shows the income potential and clients necessary to generate it, another byproduct is higher retention. Have you ever sold a product to a client, another agent came and replaced that product, and the client never reached out to you? You had not established yourself as their one-stop resource...their trusted advisor. When someone purchases the first product from you all you have is **a sale**. When you have added an additional product, now you have **a client**. But when you add that third or fourth product, which creates a comprehensive solution to their problems and needs, now you have **a raving fan.**

Raving fans call you if their circumstances change or if someone approaches them about an alternative solution or product, even if it is a product you don't represent. **That is the power of portfolio!**

Portfolio selling generates more referrals. The natural byproduct of creating raving fans is that they tell everyone about you. You have built a relationship and asking for referrals no longer feels uncomfortable because you have earned the right to gain access to their network of friends and family. The portfolio approach creates several opportunities for the Senior Insurance Advisor to interact with key people in their clients' lives. We will discuss more about that in The Selling Process section.

Generate a higher close rate. Which lead would you rather have? A cold call lead or repeat business opportunity or referral? As we will review in an upcoming section, the "holy grail" of leads is repeat business and referrals. Certainly the first product sold to a new client would be the toughest, but when you call them back, having already set the stage for the additional products the close is almost assured.

Portfolio selling creates a fluid sales cycle. As mentioned, lead generation is the challenge for most agents, and there is always an "effort phase" component, particularly for new sales people. As you build the base of clients, you should be able to transition into the "skill phase" where business is meeting you at your desk every day versus you going out and finding it. When you have a base of clients to work systematically, and continue to add in the various forms of marketing, you now have a system – a predictable model based on the science of selling. Rather than having seasonal peaks and valleys and "dead zones", portfolio selling gives you year round stability, scalability for growth and sustainability of income.

Income possibilities are exponentially greater. Certainly, there are people that take the one product approach and do quite well with it. They have a consistent lead generation and a referral process. They invest in their business and instead of being individual producers, they are running a system. The thought of adding more products is not attractive as it would detract from their core business. But for the majority who do not have the benefit of a system, portfolio selling is the fastest way to achieve six-figure income. Because it is based on a balanced portfolio of products that have various commission and renewal structures, it is easier to build a bigger base of predictable income, *even if you are starting at zero.*

The advantages of taking the portfolio approach will afford the Senior Insurance Advisor several benefits that make their business more stable, scalable and sustainable.

The 80% Sales Solution

One of the first things that agents note as a challenge to portfolio selling is that they don't want to learn so many products. Or more specifically, they don't feel *comfortable* with certain products and as a result do not offer them to their clients. Simple review of an agent's Department of Insurance records will indicate that agents do not have a shortage of carrier contracts and appointments, but they are short on the knowledge it takes to be comfortable selling them.

That is where the 80% Sales Solution concept comes in. As a matter of record, I do not like this rule as it relates to agents and their contribution to sales organizations. It is the rule that says 80% of the production will come from 20% of the sales team. I have worked in large organizations and have seen The Law of Pareto play out, but I refuse to dismiss 80% of the people just to play the mathematical odds. Many of the people in the 80% are just one ingredient away from breakout success and the job of sales organizations is to provide them access to success.

As it relates to products in your portfolio however, I am a big fan of the 80% Sales Solution. This rule states that 80% of the clients in the marketplace can be helped with 20% of the products. That is the focus we will take in building a specific product portfolio using the three core products. **This will cut down on your learning curve and help you become more comfortable with the products you sell.**

The 80% Sales Solution does mean that there are 20% of the people who will need a *different solution* than the ones you are capable of offering. That is why you are called a Senior Insurance Advisor. Nothing wrong with telling a client you don't have the best solution and pointing them in the right direction. You will never close 100% of the people you see, regardless!

Let's get ready to help the 80% majority. While this is not meant to be an exhaustive review, here is a quick summary of the 20% products you will need;

Final Expense	Medicare Supplement	Medicare Advantage	Hospital Indemnity
•5-6 contracts •Immediate •Graded •Modified (Guaranteeed Issue) •Premiums •Underwriting •Ratings	•3-4 companies •First dollar coverage Plan F only •Premium •Rate stability •Market name & presence	•3-4 national carriers w/ Part D •1-2 Strong regional players •C-SNPs & D-SNPs • Network • Benefits	•2-3 companies • Underwriting • Premium

The Products Overview

Final Expense 101

Immediate	Graded	Modified
• Full face at issue • Lowest premiums • Builds cash value • Health questions determine eligibility	• Build up to face value • Full face value at end of Graded period • Higher premiums • Builds cash value • Health questions determine eligibility	• 1st two years return of premiums paid plus interest • Full Face in 3rd year • Highest premiums • Builds cash Value • Guaranteed Issue (no medical questions)

- As with all of the products we will review there is a myriad of choices available for you the agent to represent and for the consumer to purchase. These three types of final expense insurance are selected for your core portfolio with the 80% Sales Solution in mind.

- There may be other products you decide to contract but be careful of contracting just to get one sale.

- Final expense life insurance was designed with the senior population in mind. It bridges the gap between insurability and affordability

- Most are permanent life insurance (Whole Life building cash value) and are in force as long as premiums are paid. Face amounts are lower with averages of $10,000 to $25,000 being common.

- Not designed for high face value amounts with the intention to leave a family legacy but to take care of burial costs and other final expenses.

 With many seniors underinsured/uninsured and the presence of pre-existing health conditions, Final Expense provides a solution to burial costs while providing peace of mind.

Medicare Advantage 101

- The subject of Medicare Advantage is a potentially complex one. Most of what you need to know will be taught through annual certification and testing, such as AHIP (American Health Insurance Plans).

- Certification is where you will learn the types of Medicare programs available, marketing guidelines and regulations, and the specifics of each individual carrier's products. Each Medicare Advantage carrier has their own procedure but all require certification.

- Using the 80% Sales Solution and some tools we will see in later sections you will contract with the 20% of the products that will help the vast majority of the people. Here are a few things to consider;

- **Network access** - Many seniors are already receiving care and may be very loyal to their providers. There are several Medicare Advantage plan types based on network access including HMO, PPO, RPPO and PFFS. Each has its own rules for accessing providers and the cost associated with services.

- **Special Needs Plans** - There are three categories of special needs plans – Chronic Illness (CSNP), Dual (DSNP) and Institutional (people in nursing homes). These provide additional choice, and the opportunity for year-round enrollment through special election periods (SEPs)

- **Election Periods** – There are several things and special dates that determine if and when a member can join a Medicare Advantage plan. The Annual Election Period (AEP) is the most common and occurs from October 15th – December 7th each year. As you will learn through the certification process, there are many opportunities beyond this small window for people to join or change plans.

- **Benefit designs** - What makes Medicare Advantage attractive is that it offers everything that Original Medicare offers, but then provides extra benefits such as vision, dental and hearing. The cost share structure such as co-pays and coinsurance are also favorable when compared to Original Medicare. The plan designs will vary and it will be important for the Senior Insurance Advisor to do a full review of all plans in their selected geography and to do a comparison. More information will be provided in The Sales Process section.

Remember that almost **1 in 3** people on Medicare choose Medicare Advantage. While the volume of options can be daunting, particularly for the Senior Insurance Advisor who is new to Medicare, most of what they need to learn will be taught through the certification process.

Medicare Supplement 101

Benefits	Medicare Supplement Insurance (Medigap) plans									
	A	B	C	D	F*	G	K	L	M	N
Medicare Part A coinsurance and hospital costs (up to an additional 365 days after Medicare benefits are used)	100%	100%	100%	100%	100%	100%	100%	100%	100%	100%
Medicare Part B coinsurance or copayment	100%	100%	100%	100%	100%	100%	50%	75%	100%	100% **
Blood (first 3 pints)	100%	100%	100%	100%	100%	100%	50%	75%	100%	100%
Part A hospice care coinsurance or copayment	100%	100%	100%	100%	100%	100%	50%	75%	100%	100%
Skilled nursing facility care coinsurance			100%	100%	100%	100%	50%	75%	100%	100%
Medicare Part A deductible		100%	100%	100%	100%	100%	50%	75%	50%	100%
Medicare Part B deductible			100%		100%					
Medicare Part B excess charges					100%	100%				
Foreign travel emergency (up to plan limits)			100%	100%	100%	100%			100%	100%
							Out-of-pocket limit in 2013			
							$4,800	$2,400		

- With a Medigap plan the beneficiary is essentially covered for all costs related to healthcare and in exchange for that protection pays a monthly premium. The benefits will be the same by company but premiums will differ by carrier.

- The only difference between "first dollar coverage" Plan C and Plan F is the excess charges of up to 115% for providers who do not accept Medicare Assignment. The premiums vary only slightly so Plan F offers more protection.

Due to standardization of plan design, and the benefit of "first dollar coverage" Plan F is the 80% Sales Solution option for Medicare Supplemental. The majority of consumers purchase this plan.

Hospital Indemnity 101

- The simplest of the three core products is hospital indemnity.

- The highest cost-sharing exposure for most Medicare Advantage plans is hospitalization. One inpatient stay could negate the cost savings of a zero premium plan.

- A hospital indemnity plan pays when the policy holder is hospitalized. There is no coordination of benefit so it pays in addition to what the health plan covers. The payment is also made directly to the policyholder.

- Normally covers a specific benefit period such as 10-day or 21-day.

- The amount paid per day is elected by the beneficiary at time of policy…such as $300 per day for each day of confinement up to the benefit period limits (I.E 10-days). For example, if you are hospitalized for 5 days and the daily benefit is $300, then you are eligible for a total of $1,500.

- Benefits refresh or "start over" after a certain number of consecutive days out of the hospital.

- There are minimal underwriting and pre-existing condition guidelines.

- The policy is portable regardless of what underlying healthcare the beneficiary has including Original Medicare, Medicare Advantage, Medigap, employer coverage, etc.

Hospital Indemnity creates very comprehensive coverage, particularly when added to Medicare Advantage. The premium for these policies is low especially when combined with a zero plan premium product.

Understanding the Options

The Choices That Must Be Made When Turning 65

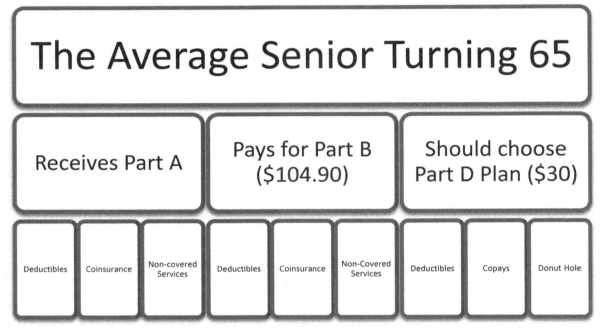

The Average Senior Turning 65

Receives Part A	Pays for Part B ($104.90)	Should choose Part D Plan ($30)
Deductibles · Coinsurance · Non-covered Services	Deductibles · Coinsurance · Non-Covered Services	Deductibles · Copays · Donut Hole

- At retirement, many beneficiaries are losing comprehensive coverage and do not understand the unpredictability and variability of the costs of Medicare.

- They are being flooded with mail, phones calls and other solicitations providing one product answers when they need more comprehensive solutions to meet their needs.

- They sign up for the basic coverage required (without incurring penalties) which leaves the beneficiary exposed to several coverage "gaps".

- Solutions sold "in a vacuum" provide additional levels of coverage and protection but may not meet the full needs of the beneficiary.

- Implemented programs should be reviewed annually to insure they still meet the evolving environment and needs of the beneficiary.

 **Educated and ethical Senior Insurance Advisors that specialize in life and healthcare options are invaluable to the process and provide protection, security and peace of mind to beneficiaries.**

The Options You Offer Are Based On Coverage Gaps

The Average Senior Turning 65

Receives Part A

Part B ($104.90)

Part D Plan ($30)

Covers:

Hospital Inpatient Care
Skilled Nursing Care
Home Healthcare
Hospice

Coverage Gaps:
Hospital
$1,216 deductible
$304 per day for days 61-90
$608 per day for days 91+

Skilled Nursing
$0 Days 1-20
$152 days 21-100

Covers:

Professional Charges to include: Physician Services, Preventive Services, Outpatient Surgery, Lab & X-rays, Ambulance Services, DME, and others

Coverage Gaps:
$147 annual deductible
20% Coinsurance

Covers:

Generic & Brand medications based on plan formulary

Coverage Gaps
(Varies by plan):
Deductible
Copayments
Initial Coverage: $0-$2,850
Coverage Gap: $2,850 - $4,550 (discounts apply)
Catastrophic: $4,550 (low copay structure applies)

<u>Uncover where the client is exposed to "gaps" and cover them with the most appropriate products.</u>

Trusted Senior Insurance Advisors sell the most comprehensive coverage the client <u>can afford</u>...*not based on premium or commission!*

The Medicare Supplement Option

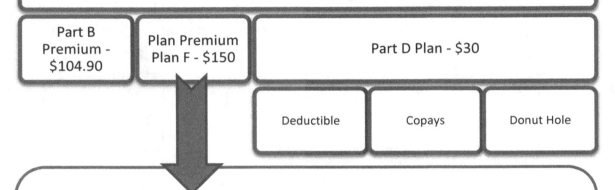

The Average Senior Turning 65

Medicare Supplement

Part B Premium - $104.90	Plan Premium Plan F - $150	Part D Plan - $30

Deductible	Copays	Donut Hole

What Plan F Covers:

- Part A & B Deductibles and Coinsurances
- 365 additional inpatient hospital days after Original Medicare benefits exhausted
- Skilled Nursing Benefit for 100 days
- Part B Excess charges (above Medicare approved to 115%)
- Foreign Travel (Emergencies) – After $250 deductible, 80% is covered up to a lifetime maximum of $50,000

If affordability is not a key driver and/or there are limited Medicare Advantage options (including non-favorable networks) then a Medigap plan is a <u>strong option.</u>

Focus on Plan F as part of the 80% Sales Solution and you can help the vast majority of supplement purchasers.

The Medicare Advantage Option

The Average Senior Turning 65

Medicare Advantage w/ Part D (MAPD)

Part B Premium - $104.90

Plan Premiums - $0

Copays/Coinsurance

Max Out of Pocket (MOOP)

Plans may charge a premium but most are $0 plan premium

Fixed copay structure for core benefits, i.e. $10 per Primary Care and $25 for Specialist visit

Highest copay is usually inpatient hospital with a per day copay, i.e. $250 per day for days 1-5

May also cover additional benefits and services to include: Routine vision/ eyewear, dental/dentures, hearing/hearing aids, worldwide emergencies and other benefits

This is an upper limit on how much members pay "out of pocket" for Part A B services received during a calendar year (does not include Part D costs. Once reached, the plan pays 100% of all costs associated with Part A & Part B services. Current CMS maximum is $6.700

The cost favorability (premiums and cost-sharing) of Medicare Advantage make it an attractive option for many beneficiaries.

There are certain illnesses (i.e. radiation/chemotherapy) and hospitalization which can be covered with other products in the Senior Insurance Advisors Portfolio.

A Quick Comparison of the Three Healthcare Options

The average senior turning 65

Option 1	Option 2	Option 3
Original Medicare w/Stand Alone Part D	Original Medicare w Medigap and Stand Alone Part D	Medicare Advantage (MAPD)
Monthly Fixed Cost $134.90	Monthly Fixed Cost $284.90	Monthly Fixed Cost $104.90
Annual Fixed Cost $1,618.80	Annual fixed Cost $3,418.80	Annual Fixed Cost $1,258.80
Medical Cost Share Exposure Unlimited (Highest)	Medical Cost Share Exposure 3,418.80 (Lowest)	Medical Cost Share Exposure $7,958.80 (MOOP)

- For the moment do not consider the above chart as a hierarchy of choice. Each of the three healthcare scenarios have their pros and cons largely rooted in cost exposure, networking provider access, and availability.

- If you are not accustomed to selling based on the best fit approach, do not default to your normal way of business but prepare for a paradigm shift and seeing these products in a new way.

- While there are many more scenarios in the "real world" we are going to continue to evaluate the options through the 80% Sales Solution approach. That may mean referring some clients to other professionals for the best solution but will allow you to assist the vast majority of beneficiaries.

The Power of Hospital Indemnity

The Realization of Hospitalization

Medicare Advantage Inpatient Hospital Costs Sample				
Medicare Advantage Plan	Copay Per Day	# Of Days	Co-pay per admission*	OOP Max
Plan B	$255	1-4	$900	$4,900
Plan C	$250	1-7	$1,250	$5,900
Plan D	$395	1-4	$1,975	$6,700
*Average LOS (Length of Stay) is 5 days				

- The single greatest co-pay for the majority of Medicare Advantage plans is inpatient hospital cost. They are normally designed to be a fixed cost per day for a specific number of days. This structure is favorable and allows for the predictability of cost in the event of hospitalization.

- The downside is the possibility of multiple admissions and the additional cost that may be incurred. The Out Of Pocket Max (MOOP) provides an ultimate upper limit of protection, but is still exposure many beneficiaries want to cover.

- There are other costs associated with hospitalization that healthcare coverage does not address and will have a financial impact on the beneficiary.

- Even with healthy Medicare beneficiaries, there is still a greater sense of mortality and the inevitability of hospitalization at some point, whether it be elective or urgent. It is no longer a question of "if" but more a question of "when".

- While zero premium Medicare advantage is attractive from a monthly fixed cost perspective, remember that beneficiaries want the most comprehensive coverage they can afford.

- That is where Hospital Indemnity comes in as a valuable part of the Senior Insurance Advisor portfolio.

For most Medicare beneficiaries, hospitalization is not a question of "if"…but "when" and the associated costs are a concern. Hospital Indemnity can provide additional financial protection and peace of mind.

Adding the Protection of Hospital Indemnity

The Average Senior Turning 65

Medicare Advantage	Hospital Indemnity Policy

Part B Premium - $104.90	Plan Premiums $0 - $70*	Copays	Donut Hole	Policy Premium - $30

For this example;

10-day benefit period (defines up to the number of days payable)

$250 per day (to match the inpatient copay of the Medicare Advantage plan)

No coordination of benefit with any plan (including Medicare, Medigap, or Medicare Advantage) and is paid in addition to other insurance

Pays the beneficiary directly

Adding Hospital Indemnity to a Medicare Advantage plan (particularly zero premium plans) is a great benefit to the beneficiary creating more comprehensive, cost-effective coverage.

Going Deeper Into Indemnity

Original Medicare Only

	Traditional Medicare Only
Monthly Premiums	Part B – 104.90 Part D - $30
Monthly Cost	$134.90
Annual Plan Cost	**$1,618.80**
Hospital Cost (5 day LOS)	$1,216*
Annual Cost w/Hosp Stay	**$2,834.80**
Indemnity Payment to beneficiary	$0 (no coverage)
Net Cost	**$2,802.80**
The difference between planned "fixed" costs and actual costs	**($1,216.00)**
	* For this illustration, Part B deductible and 20% coinsurance not part of cost

- To get a baseline we have to look at original Medicare in a vacuum. The fixed cost of Medicare is less than half the cost of Medigap and on par with the cost of most Medicare advantage plans.

- While it provides much more coverage than having no health insurance, the coverage gaps we just reviewed leaves the beneficiary greatly exposed to unpredictable high cost.

- The deductibles and 20% coinsurance for a healthy individual are manageable, but for someone diagnosed with a chronic illness or ongoing medical treatment that exposure can be devastating.

There is no circumstance, except in *extreme* financial challenge, <u>and</u> the absence of geographic choice that someone should be left with the option of Original Medicare only.

Original Medicare with Indemnity

	Traditional Medicare Only	Traditional Medicare w/ Indemnity
Monthly Premiums	Part B – 104.90 Part D - $30	Part B – 104.90 Part D - $30 Indemnity - $30**
Monthly Cost	$134.90	$164.90
Annual Plan Cost	**$1,618.80**	**$1,978.80**
Hospital Cost (5 day LOS)	$1,216*	$1,216*
Annual Cost w/Hosp Stay	**$2,834.80**	**$3,194.80**
Indemnity Payment to beneficiary	$0 (no coverage)	$1,250
Net Cost	**$2,802.80**	**$1,944.80**
The difference between planned "fixed" costs and actual costs	**($1,216.00)**	**$34**
	* For this illustration, Part B deductible and 20% coinsurance not part of cost of Original Medicare	* Hospital Indemnity - $250 per day with 10-day benefit period in all illustrations

- Original Medicare *with* a Hospital Indemnity policy is a great option when Medigap affordability presents a problem and there are no viable Medicare Advantage options available geographically.

- As with final expense policies the Senior Insurance Advisor can "zero in" on both the day rate and duration based on the premium the beneficiary can afford.

- If no Medigap or Medicare Advantage is in place, then the highest day rate affordable should be chosen to help offset original Medicare deductibles and coinsurance.

- Since there is no coordination of benefits any additional payment the beneficiary receives can be used for other important expenses, such as Part B gaps.

- Depending on the carrier there may be pre-existing conditions and length of time since last hospitalization that may prevent the beneficiary from obtaining coverage.

 Hospital Indemnity should <u>always</u> be reviewed as a potential option based on beneficiary lifestyle and needs.

Original Medicare Options vs. Medigap

	Traditional Medicare Only	Traditional Medicare w/ Indemnity	Medicare w/ Medigap Policy
Monthly Premiums	Part B – 104.90 Part D - $30	Part B – 104.90 Part D - $30 Indemnity - $30**	Part B – 104.90 Part D - $30 Medigap - $150***
Monthly Cost	$134.90	$164.90	$284.90
Annual Plan Cost	**$1,618.80**	**$1,978.80**	**$3,418.80**
Hospital Cost (5 day LOS)	$1,216*	$1,216*	$0
Annual Cost w/Hosp Stay	**$2,834.80**	**$3,194.80**	**$3,418.80**
Indemnity Payment to beneficiary	$0 (no coverage)	$1,250	$0 (no coverage)
Net Cost	**$2,802.80**	**$1,944.80**	**$3,418.80**
The difference between planned "fixed" costs and actual costs	**($1,216.00)**	**$34**	**$0**
	* For this illustration, Part B deductible and 20% coinsurance not part of cost of Original Medicare	** Hospital Indemnity - $250 per day with 10-day benefit period in all illustrations	*** Plan F rate from Medicare.gov premium range for zip code 30236 Georgia

- Original Medicare with a Medigap policy is already *very comprehensive*, particularly if it is a first dollar coverage plan, such as Plan F.

- It provides the highest security of coverage for a fixed predictable monthly payment. In this example, compare the fixed cost of $3400 annually against the potential of runaway expenses for original Medicare and even against the Maximum Out Of Pocket for Medicare Advantage of $6700 (as limited by CMS).

- Premiums can and usually do increase on an annual basis but provide the stability of standardized coverage not available with the annually changing potential of Medicare Advantage plans.

- Hospital Indemnity can be used with Medigap as an additional source of financial assistance *but only if the needs and lifestyle of the beneficiary require it.*

First dollar Medigap policies (Plan F) are comprehensive coverage and Hospital Indemnity should only be sold based on beneficiary needs and lifestyle. Any additional available funds may be better utilized in other areas.

Original Medicare Options vs. Medigap vs. Advantage Only

	Traditional Medicare Only	Traditional Medicare w/ Indemnity	Medicare w/ Medigap Policy	Medicare Advantage Only
Monthly Premiums	Part B – 104.90 Part D - $30	Part B – 104.90 Part D - $30 Indemnity - $30**	Part B – 104.90 Part D - $30 Medigap - $150***	Part B – 104.90 Part D - $30 MAPD - $0
Monthly Cost	$134.90	$164.90	$284.90	$134.90
Annual Plan Cost	**$1,618.80**	**$1,978.80**	**$3,418.80**	**$1,618.80**
Hospital Cost (5 day LOS)	$1,216*	$1,216*	$0	$1,250****
Annual Cost w/Hosp Stay	**$2,834.80**	**$3,194.80**	**$3,418.80**	**$2,868.80**
Indemnity Payment to beneficiary	$0 (no coverage)	$1,250	$0 (no coverage)	$0 (no coverage)
Net Cost	**$2,802.80**	**$1,944.80**	**$3,418.80**	**$2,868.80**
The difference between planned "fixed" costs and actual costs	($1,216.00)	$34	$0	($1,250)
	* For this illustration, Part B deductible and 20% coinsurance not part of cost of Original Medicare	* *Hospital Indemnity - $250 per day with 10-day benefit period in all illustrations	*** Plan F rate from Medicare.gov premium range for zip code 30236 Georgia	**** Plan has inpatient copay of $250 per day for days 1-7

- How comprehensive and cost-effective a Medicare Advantage plan is can only be determined by its benefits. While zero premium is most attractive, if there are high co-pays and coinsurance for needed services then that favorability is minimized.

- Due largely to reimbursement, which can be driven geographically and through revenue optimization at a health plan level, there are some markets that have extremely rich benefits and others that are more basic.

- While our focus has been mainly on zero premium options, there are good choices that do have a monthly plan premium that should also be reviewed by the advisor.

- It is only when the monthly plan premium, along with benefit design, network access and Maximum Out of Pocket begin approaching the cost of a Medigap policy that the decision becomes less obvious.

- In examining the Annual Plan Cost of Original Medicare and Medicare Advantage Only, we see that they are equal at $1600. In the event of a hospitalization they are also very close to parity. While this example does not include the 20% (Part B gaps), if the hospital stay is five days, the cost of original Medicare and Medicare Advantage are in the same range.

- Medicare Advantage retains its favorability over original Medicare because of the Maximum Out Of Pocket provision to keep costs from running away even in the event of a catastrophic illness.

- Original Medicare with Indemnity begins to close that gap for hospitalization occurrences.

Medicare Advantage is a strong option where the combination of monthly premium, network access, cost share structure and **MOOP** work together to build the best fit option for the beneficiary.

It is the job of the Senior Insurance Advisor to help the beneficiary determine which plan option is the best fit.

Original Medicare Options *vs.* Medigap *vs.* Advantage Options

	Traditional Medicare Only	Traditional Medicare w/ Indemnity	Medicare w/ Medigap Policy	Medicare Advantage Only	Medicare Advantage w/ Indemnity
Monthly Premiums	Part B – 104.90 Part D - $30	Part B – 104.90 Part D - $30 Indemnity - $30**	Part B – 104.90 Part D - $30 Medigap - $150***	Part B – 104.90 Part D - $30 MAPD - $0	Part B – 104.90 Part D - $30 MAPD - $0 Indemnity - $30**
Monthly Cost	$134.90	$164.90	$284.90	$134.90	$164.90
Annual Plan Cost	$1,618.80	$1,978.80	$3,418.80	$1,618.80	$1,978.80
Hospital Cost (5 day LOS)	$1,216*	$1,216*	$0	$1,250****	$1,250****
Annual Cost w/Hosp Stay	$2,834.80	$3,194.80	$3,418.80	$2,868.80	$3,228.80
Indemnity Payment to beneficiary	$0 (no coverage)	$1,250	$0 (no coverage)	$0 (no coverage)	$1,250
Net Cost	$2,802.80	$1,944.80	$3,418.80	$2,868.80	$1978.80
The difference between planned "fixed" costs and actual costs	($1,216.00)	$34	$0	($1,250)	$0
	* For this illustration, Part B deductible and 20% coinsurance not part of cost of Original Medicare	**Hospital Indemnity - $250 per day with 10-day benefit period in all illustrations	*** Plan F rate from Medicare.gov premium range for zip code 30236 Georgia	**** Plan has inpatient copay of $250 per day for days 1-7	

- For our last comparison, we add Hospital Indemnity to a zero plan premium Medicare Advantage. From a purely financial perspective it is the strongest option of the five;
    - It has the lowest net cost of all our scenarios at $1980.
    - It provides $250 a day for up to 10 days and the benefit "restores" and begins fresh after the prescribed days of non-confinement based on the provisions of the policy.
    - Since there is no coordination of benefits all cost incurred as copayment for the hospitalization accrue toward the Maximum Out Of Pocket. Each payment received from the policy can offset the cost of care but also count toward that maximum.
- The Annual Plan Cost of Medicare Advantage with Indemnity is only $360 more than original Medicare by itself and is $1500 less than the Medigap.

- Regardless of that prescribed and defined process a Senior Insurance Advisor must include Indemnity in EVERY healthcare scenario even if it requires a subsequent visit.

When the beneficiary can meet the underwriting provisions, and the premium cost are weighed against the cost-sharing exposure, then Hospital Indemnity becomes a vital component of the Senior Insurance Advisors portfolio...*particularly when combined with Medicare Advantage.*

Section 2 Summary

Section Two Summary

- It takes 3 Core Products to create the Senior Insurance Advisor portfolio: Final Expense Life Insurance, Medicare Supplemental/Medicare Advantage and Hospital Indemnity.

- The benefits of selling multiple products culminate in the Senior Insurance Advisor becoming the "one stop" Trusted Advisor.

- The complex product offerings can be greatly simplified with the 80% Sales Solution. Choosing the "vital few" products that can impact the greatest number of clients with best fit solutions.

- The best product for marketing is Final Expense and the marketing opportunities generated by portfolio selling create year-round sustainable sales cycles.

- Upon retirement or disability, Medicare only beneficiaries are exposed to several "gaps" and desire comprehensive coverage they can afford necessitating a series of advisors or one portfolio advisor.

- Reviewing the healthcare scenarios, the Senior Insurance Advisor should leverage the full range of healthcare and insurance options to build the best fit plan for their clients.

- One size does not fit all and each scenario presents a unique situation for the Senior Insurance Advisor to analyze and provide viable options.

- Hospital Indemnity can provide much needed additional financial protection based on the needs and lifestyle of the client.

- The ethical and educated Senior Insurance Advisor will take the additional steps necessary to remain compliant and at the same time meet the needs of their clients.

- The Senior Insurance Advisor can build a high six-figure income in an environment of service to a needing and deserving population so again, *"As you serve...you deserve"*

End of Section Two

SECTION NOTES

_____

_____

_____

_____

_____

_____

_____

_____

_____

_____

_____

_____

_____

_____

_____

_____

_____

_____

_____

SECTION NOTES

SECTION NOTES

Section 3: The Financial Opportunity

Time Required: 30 Minutes

Time Remaining: 4 Hours 00 Minutes

What you will learn in this session;

25 min	Product by Product Commission Review
5 min	The Power of Putting Them All Together
120 min	Running Time

Commissions are a complex and sensitive topic. Commissions are an important component of the Senior Insurance Advisors business model, but be aware that commissions may vary from company to company, product to product, and agency to agency. Any discussion on commissions will invite debate and send agents looking for "a few dollars more". You should view commissions as a "total package", and not just from a single product perspective, much like a mutual fund manager views a basket of stocks.

While there is a great range in commission, with the exception of Medicare Advantage (which is essentially standardized), the variances will normally be based on your production and experience.

- On the lower end of the commission scale;

    o Are you new to the business and needing training, development and mentoring?

    o Are you receiving leads, marketing assistance and other forms of business support?

    o Are you a captive agent?

    o Are you lacking a proven track record of production?

- At the higher end of the commission scale;

    o Do you have a proven record of production and years of experience?

    o Are you capable of generating your own leads without any form of support from your agency?

    o Do you have a higher than acceptable persistency rate to protect your agency from unpredictable chargebacks?

    o Do you have a structured group of agents and running them with minimal business assistance (i.e. administrative)?

    o Do you have multiple products with the same agency, giving them a better chance through broader production and products?

Until you have proven production experience, expect to be on the lower end of commission opportunities during your "effort phase". Pay your dues, review/honor your contracts and grow your revenue through excellence in service to your clients as a trusted Senior Insurance Advisor.

Final Expense Commission

Final Expense Commission Scenarios
Immediate Benefit & Graded Whole Life Policies
$40 Commissionable Monthly Premium

Commission Level	50%	60%	70%	80%	90%	100%	115%
Total Commission	$240	$288	$336	$384	$432	$480	$552
75% Advance	$180	$216	$252	$288	$324	$360	$414
Remaining 1st year *(paid out over 3 months)*	$20 x 3 = $60	$24 x 3 = $74	$28 x 3 = $84	$32 x 3 = $96	$36 x 3 = $108	$40 x 3 = $120	$46 x 3 = $138
1st Year Commission If Paid "As Earned" *(Monthly)*	$20 x 12 = $240	$24 x 12 = $288	$28 x 12 = $336	$32 x 12 = $384	$36 x12 = $432	$40 x 12 = $480	$46 x 12 = $552

Renewals (Based on 115% Contract)

Years	2-5	6-10	11+
Commission Level	6.25%	4.50%	1.40%
Annual Amount	$30.00	$21.60	$6.72
Monthly As Earned Payment	$2.50	$1.80	$0.56

- Final Expense is a great foundational product that has tremendous first year potential of commission. If the company advances, then that provides great cash flow to your business.

- Renewals in year two and beyond drop off considerably but still provide revenue and a servicing opportunity with the clientele for additional products and referrals.

- Essentially every person you meet is a candidate for life insurance, thus creating a great marketing platform.

- There is limited compliance and regulatory constraints, as compared to Medicare products, which allows for a broader, more cost-effective lead generation and business development approach.

- Once the Senior Insurance Advisor reaches a certain revenue level on a monthly basis, "as earned" commission on new sales can be an attractive option.

Final Expense Commission Scenarios
Modified & Guaranteed Issue Whole Life Policies
$40 Commissionable Monthly Premium

Commission Level	40%	45%	50%	55%
Total Commission	$192	$216	$240	$264
75% Advance	$144	$162	$180	$198
Remaining 1st year *(paid out over 3 months)*	$16 x 3 = $48	$18 x 3 = $54	$20 x 3 = $60	$22 x 3 = $66
1st Year Commission If Paid "As Earned" *(Monthly)*	$16 x 12 = $192	$18 x 12 = $216	$20 x 12 = $240	$22 x 12 = $264

Renewals (Based on 55% Contract)

Years	2-5	6-10	11+
Commission Level	3.25%	2.50%	1.40%
Annual Amount	$15.60	$12.00	$6.72
Monthly As Earned Payment	$1.30	$1.00	$0.56

- Modified and guaranteed issue policies come with much higher risk to the insurer and thus the commission levels are essentially half of other policies.

- Correspondingly, the premiums to the policyholder are usually much higher and create a similar commission opportunity to other Final Expense products.

- Many of these policies are paid as earned, but there are companies that advance.

- Guaranteed issue policies should only be used when no other underwritten policy with lower premiums can be obtained.

- Because there are no medical questions and no underwriting, these policies are in some cases the only option to obtain insurance. There is a great need for these types of policies to help people with their final expenses.

Final Expense provides a great cash flow opportunity through high commission percentages and advances. The universal need for the product also creates a platform from which to market the other products in the portfolio. The Senior Insurance Advisor should endeavor to serve all clients and "As you serve...you deserve".

Hospital Indemnity

Hospital Indemnity
$40 Commissionable Monthly Premium

Commission Level	40%	45%	50%	55%
Total Commission	$192	$216	$240	$264
75% Advance	$144	$162	$180	$198
Remaining 1st year *(paid out over 3 months)*	$16 x 3 = $48	$18 x 3 = $54	$20 x 3 = $60	$22 x 3 = $66
1st Year Commission If Paid "As Earned" *(Monthly)*	$16 x 12 = $192	$18 x 12 = $216	$20 x 12 = $240	$22 x 12 = $264

Renewals (Based on 55% Contract)

Years	2-10	11+
Commission Level	8%	4%
Annual Amount	$38.40	$19.20
Monthly As Earned Payment	$3.20	$1.60

- Like guaranteed issue in the previous chart, hospital indemnity products generally pay about half the commission of immediate issue final expense products.

- This is due largely to the fact that a benefit paying event (hospitalization) will occur and could occur multiple times. Generally, the premiums are reasonable and these products provide additional protection for your clients.

- First year commission opportunity is still on par with Medicare Advantage. Year two and beyond, provide a small amount of additional revenue each month.

- Many of these policies are paid as earned, but there are companies that do advance.

- As we reviewed in the previous section, hospital indemnity is a logical extension of Medicare Advantage and ultimately "sells itself" when presented in proper fashion.

At a minimum, Hospital Indemnity sales will double the income opportunity (1st year commissions) for agents that predominately/exclusively sell Medicare Advantage and create another avenue to obtain repeat business and referrals.

Medicare Supplement Commission Table

Medicare Supplemental $150 Monthly/$1,800 Annual Commissionable Premium Plan F	
1st Year Commission Level	18%
1st Year Commission Payment	$324
Years 2-6 Commission Level	18%
Years 2-6 Commission Payment	$324
Years 7-10 Commission Level	7%
Years 11+	N/A

- Medicare Supplements are products that generate high first-year commission potential, and typically, years two through six are level payments that equal the first year.

- This mirrors the payment philosophy of Medicare Advantage and provides even further incentive for the Senior Insurance Advisor to sell the product that is the best fit.

- Commissions based on percentages are usually calculated on initial premium, and does not change if there are annual increases in premium charged to the beneficiary.

- The commission percentage level encompasses a wide range and some carriers pay dollar rates versus percentages.

- Beyond this very simple example of a Plan F commission structure, there are numerous iterations of payments based on age, plan type, open enrollment/guaranteed issue periods, replacement, etc.

- Because Medicare Supplemental requires a Part D plan, there will be an additional small commission for writing the pharmacy plan.

Medicare Supplements provide great revenue opportunity and cash flow, particularly years 1-6 with level payments. Building a base of clients generates stable income from which to build and expand the business of a Senior Insurance Advisor.

Medicare Advantage Commission

Since the **Medicare Improvements for Patients and Providers Act of 2008** (MIPPA) instituted a form of "standardized" commission structures for brokers, there have been several iterations and changes. Prior to this act, commissions were set by the carriers and amounts paid could vary widely.

The positive aspects of the Act include; higher payments for initial enrollments (first-timers), structured renewal payments (many carriers pay lifetime level payments), and it essentially created a level playing field carrier to carrier. While the structures outlined below require review to understand, the revenue opportunity presented by Medicare Advantage is still *very attractive*.

In these three charts, we are ultimately reviewing two possible scenarios;

1. The beneficiary you enroll is moving from one MAPD plan to another – *considered a Renewal Enrollment for purposes of payment.*

2. The beneficiary you enroll is coming to a MA plan for the first time, such as aging into Medicare (turning 65 or obtaining Medicare through Disability) - *considered an Initial Enrollment for purposes of payment.*

A few points about commission before we review examples;

- There is a predefined payment structure set by the Centers for Medicare and Medicaid Services (CMS) that governs broker payment. The current structure of Initial Payment and Renewal Payment is 2:1. This means if a carrier sets its Initial Payment at the CMS maximum (the amount differs by geography), then Renewal Payments have to be 50% of that amount. There is current discussion and proposals about reducing Renewal Payments to 35% of the Initial Payment.

- Our charts use an Initial Payment max of $425, thus Renewal Payments have to be 50% of that amount or $212.50. Carriers have the option to pay less than the CMS maximum, but must maintain the 2:1 methodology.

- Carriers have the option of advancing commissions based on the charts below, or of paying as earned. For simplicity, the illustrations and charts use a maximum payment of $425 and a renewal payment of $213 (rounded).

- **Renewals are paid level through 6 years and many carriers now pay lifetime level renewal payments.**

- The scenarios below represent how most carriers will pay commissions but may be different based on several factors. **Review your contracts and commission exhibits to determine exactly how a specific carrier pays.**

Members Switching Plans & Renewal Payments

Renewal Member 1st Payment Methodology				
Effective Date	Months Enrolled	1st Payment Formula	1st Payment	Renewals Payment
January 1	12/12	(12/12) x $213	$213.00	Regardless of member effective date, the renewal period begins in January of each year
February 1	11/12	(11/12) x $213	$195.25	
March 1	10/12	(10/12) x $213	$177.50	
April 1	9/12	(9/12) x $213	$159.75	
May 1	8/12	(8/12) x $213	$142.00	
June 1	7/12	(7/12) x $213	$124.25	Advancing Carriers will pay $213.00 in January
July 1	6/12	(6/12) x $213	$106.50	
August 1	5/12	(5/12) x $213	$ 88.75	
September 1	4/12	(4/12) x $213	$ 71.00	Non-Advancing Carriers will pay $17.75 a month
October 1	3/12	(3/12) x $213	$ 53.25	
November 1	2/12	(2/12) x $213	$ 35.50	
December 1	1/12	(1/12) x $213	$ 17.75	

- This chart represents the foundation payment for all scenarios. Until a carrier is notified by CMS that a member is an Initial Enrollment, and a "Second Payment" (commonly referred to as True Up payment) is due, the carrier will pay the amount represented above.

- Based on recent broker's commission revisions, the total amount paid in first year will be determined by the enrollment effective date. Example from chart above;

  o If a member is effective May 1 and the carrier pays a renewal level of $213 then the prorated payment due the agent is $142.

  o The carrier can advance the full amount of $142 or $17.75 on monthly as earned basis.

  o If this beneficiary has an exercisable election period and is moving from one Medicare Advantage plan to another, then the $142 represents the entire payment due.

- Based on recent changes, Renewal Payments for all members regardless of their effective month, will begin in January of each year.

- In January, carriers have the option to advance full year renewal or pay as earned. To continue the example;

  o The agent enrolled the beneficiary effective May 1 and received an advanced payment of $142.

  o In January of the next year the agent receives an advanced renewal payment of $213.

  o **Total payments of $355 through the period (9 months) based on advance payments.**

Members Joining Medicare Advantage for the First Time

Initial Year 1st & 2nd Payment Methodology						
Effective Date	Months Enrolled	1st Payment	2nd Payment Formula	2nd Payment	Total	Renewal Payment
January 1	12/12	$213.00	$425 – 1st payment	$212.00	$425.00	Regardless of member effective date, the renewal period begins in January of each year
February 1	11/12	$195.25	$425 – 1st payment	$229.75	$425.00	
March 1	10/12	$177.50	$425 – 1st payment	$247.50	$425.00	
April 1	9/12	$159.75	$425 – 1st payment	$265.25	$425.00	
May 1	8/12	$142.00	$425 – 1st payment	$283.00	$425.00	
June 1	7/12	$124.25	$425 – 1st payment	$300.75	$425.00	Advancing Carriers will pay $213.00 in January
July 1	6/12	$106.50	$425 – 1st payment	$318.50	$425.00	
August 1	5/12	$ 88.75	$425 – 1st payment	$336.25	$425.00	
September 1	4/12	$ 71.00	$425 – 1st payment	$354.00	$425.00	
October 1	3/12	$ 53.25	$425 – 1st payment	$371.75	$425.00	Non-Advancing Carriers will pay $17.75 a month
November 1	2/12	$ 35.50	$425 – 1st payment	$389.50	$425.00	
December 1	1/12	$ 17.75	$425 – 1st payment	$407.25	$425.00	

- This chart represents the beneficiaries that are joining Medicare Advantage for the **first time** (as determined by CMS) but generally includes;

  o Those aging into Medicare (turning 65).

  o Beneficiaries over 65 joining Medicare Advantage for the first time.

  o Disabled people joining Medicare Advantage for the first time.

  o Medigap policyholders (regardless of age) joining Medicare Advantage for the first time.

- The upper limit of this payment is 100% of carrier commission structure not to exceed the allowable CMS maximum payment, in this example $425.

- **There is no pro-ration for these payments regardless of effective date.** However, the carrier has the option to advance the full payment or pay it monthly, but the total payment will be the same over the time period. Example from chart above;

  o If a member is effective May 1 and is joining Medicare Advantage for the first time (Initial Enrollment) the carrier will make the 1st payment of $142.

  o Once CMS has confirmed the beneficiary is Initial, the carrier will make the 2nd payment (commonly referred to as True Up payment) of $283.

  o In January of next year the agent receives an advanced renewal payment of $213.

  o **Total payments of $638 through the period (9 months) based on advance payments.**

Members in their 1st Year Changing Plans

Initial Year, Plan Switch 1st & 2nd Payment Methodology						
Effective Date	Months Enrolled	1st Payment	2nd Payment Formula	2nd Payment	Total	Renewals
January 1	12/12	$213.00	$425 x (12/12)	$212.00	$425.00	Regardless of member effective date, the renewal period begins in January of each year
February 1	11/12	$195.25	$425 x (11/12)	$194.33	$389.58	
March 1	10/12	$177.50	$425 x (10/12)	$176.67	$354.17	
April 1	9/12	$159.75	$425 x (9/12)	$159.00	$318.75	
May 1	8/12	$142.00	$425 x (8/12)	$141.33	$283.33	
June 1	7/12	$124.25	$425 x (7/12)	$123.67	$247.92	
July 1	6/12	$106.50	$425 x (6/12)	$106.00	$212.50	Advancing Carriers will pay $213.00 in January
August 1	5/12	$ 88.75	$425 x (5/12)	$ 88.33	$177.08	
September 1	4/12	$ 71.00	$425 x (4/12)	$ 70.67	$141.67	
October 1	3/12	$ 53.25	$425 x (3/12)	$ 53.00	$106.25	Non-Advancing Carriers will pay $17.75 a month
November 1	2/12	$ 35.50	$425 x (2/12)	$ 35.33	$ 70.83	
December 1	1/12	$ 17.75	$425 x (1/12)	$ 17.67	$ 35.42	

- The final scenario outlines a beneficiary who is still within the <u>first 12 months of their Initial Period</u> (joining Medicare Advantage for the first time) but has the ability through a Special Elections Period (SEP) <u>to change plans</u>. For example;

   o A beneficiary turns 65 and selects their first Medicare advantage plan for January 1st. If they have an exercisable election (SEP), such as a qualifying chronic illness, they can join a C-SNP. If the second plan is for May effective, then the agent enrolling them in the second plan receives the following payments;

   o The carrier will make the 1st payment of $142.

   o Once CMS has confirmed the beneficiary is within the first 12 months of being an Initial Enrollment, the carrier will make the 2nd payment of $141.33.

   o The total payment paid is 283.33. This is the maximum contracted payment for Initial Enrollments of $425 prorated for 8 months. ($425 x 8/12 = 283.33)

   o In January of next year the agent receives an advanced renewal payment of $213.

   o **Total payments of $496.33 through the period (9 months) based on advance payments.**

Chargebacks

- If a beneficiary dis-enrolls from a plan, there will be a chargeback assessed to the agent based on how the agent was paid (advanced or pro-rated) and whether or not the disenrollment was rapid;

   o A full chargeback is assessed when an enrollment terminates within the first three months of the enrollee's effective date. Essentially, a member must have 4 months of membership or full chargeback is assessed, whether advanced or prorated all monies are charged back.

- o A prorated chargeback is assessed when an enrollment terminates after month four.

- Chargebacks on advanced renewal payments will be prorated based on actual number of months the beneficiary was effective or renewal payments will simply stop, if paid as earned.

Summary of Medicare Advantage Commission Examples with Effective Date of May 1st			
	Changing plans	Joining plan for 1st time	1st year changing plans
1st Payment	$142	$142	$142
2nd Payment	None due	$283	$141.33
Total Payment	$142	$425	$283.33
Renewal Payment - January	$213	$213	$213
Cash Flow May - January	**$355**	**$638**	**$496.33**
		Great Revenue Opportunity	

Medicare Advantage payments allow the Senior Insurance Advisor to build a strong revenue base while serving 30% of the Medicare eligible base with largely a zero premium plan product.

Proposed changes to compensation will do little to diminish the beneficiary demand and still allow the ethical and educated advisor to build a sustainable business.

From a marketing and profitability standpoint the Senior Insurance Advisor should focus on the single largest population - people turning 65, which also represents the greatest revenue opportunity.

Medicare Advantage, Medigap & Final Expense Commission Comparison

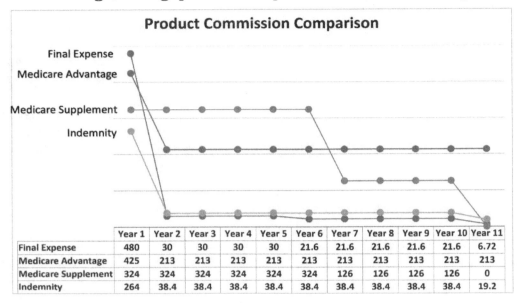

	Year 1	Year 2	Year 3	Year 4	Year 5	Year 6	Year 7	Year 8	Year 9	Year 10	Year 11
Final Expense	480	30	30	30	30	21.6	21.6	21.6	21.6	21.6	6.72
Medicare Advantage	425	213	213	213	213	213	213	213	213	213	213
Medicare Supplement	324	324	324	324	324	324	126	126	126	126	0
Indemnity	264	38.4	38.4	38.4	38.4	38.4	38.4	38.4	38.4	38.4	19.2

- This chart illustrates the first year revenue opportunity for all products in the Senior Insurance Advisor portfolio and additionally years 2 through 11.

- Depending on monthly premium and commission level, Final Expense represents the best first year opportunity but then drops off substantially years two and beyond.

- Medicare Advantage provides great first year opportunity, particularly for Initial Enrollments (first-timers to Medicare Advantage) and a strong year to year renewal payment...in many cases lifetime level renewal payments.

- Medicare Supplements also provide strong first year payments and additionally, years two through six with level payments.

- Indemnity provides substantial "add on" revenue, particularly when added to Medicare Advantage.

From a revenue standpoint, each product has its pros and cons based on various factors. In a single product approach an agent can make a good living, but when combined in a synergistic portfolio approach these core products allow the Senior Insurance Advisor to build a stable, scalable and sustainable business in the <u>high six-figure category</u>.

The Power of Putting Them All Together

Senior Insurance Advisor Portfolio Approach				
	Final Expense Foundation Product	**Medicare Supplement** (20% Of Clients Purchase)	**Medicare Advantage** (30% Of Clients Purchase)	**Hospital Indemnity** (30% Of Clients Purchase)
Total Clients	150	30	45	45
Revenue Opportunity				
	Final Expense	Medicare Supplement	Medicare Advantage	Indemnity	Total
Year 1	$57,600	$10,920	$12,765	$11,880	$93,165
Year 2	New $57,600 Renewal $4,500	New $10,920 Renewal $10,920	New $12,765 Renewal $9,585	New $11,880 Renewal $1,710	$119,880
Year 3	New $57,600 Renewal $9,000	New $10,920 Renewal $21,840	New $12,765 Renewal $19,170	New $11,880 Renewal $3,420	$146,595
Year 4	New $57,600 Renewal $13,500	New $10,920 Renewal $32,760	New $12,765 Renewal $28,755	New $11,880 Renewal $5,130	$173,310
Year 5	New $57,600 Renewal $18,000	New $10,920 Renewal $43,680	New $12,765 Renewal $38,340	New $11,880 Renewal $6,840	$200,025
Year 6	New $57,600 Renewal $22,500	New $10,920 Renewal $54,600	New $12,765 Renewal $47,925	New $11,880 Renewal $8,550	$226,740

Section 3 Summary

Section Three Summary

- You should view commissions as a "total package" and not just from a single product perspective much like a mutual fund manager views a basket of stocks.

- Review, understand and honor all of your contracts.

- Until you have proven production experience, expect to be on the lower end of commission opportunities during your "effort phase". Pay your dues, review/honor your contracts and grow your revenue through excellence in service to your clients as a trusted Senior Insurance Advisor.

- Final Expense has great 1st year potential and provides cash flow to undergird your marketing efforts.

- Medicare products represent a great 1st year payment, but real power is in 6 year renewal cycle.

- Many Medicare Advantage carriers now pay level lifetime renewals.

- At a minimum, Hospital Indemnity sales will double the income opportunity (1st year commissions) for agents that predominately/exclusively sell Medicare Advantage and create another avenue to obtain repeat business and referrals.

- The most profitable Medicare Advantage client is one who is new to Medicare (aging in). They are also growing at a rate of 10,000 a day and provide the best marketing opportunity.

- Each product alone can provide a true opportunity for success.

- Combined in a portfolio, these core products will provide the Senior Insurance Advisor a tremendous Six-Figure income opportunity.

End of Section Three

SECTION NOTES

_____

_____

_____

_____

_____

_____

_____

_____

_____

_____

_____

_____

_____

_____

_____

_____

_____

_____

SECTION NOTES

Section 4: Securing Clients

Time Required: I Hour 30 Minutes

Time Remaining: 2 Hours 30 minutes

What you will learn in this session;

5 min	Finding Your Audience and Building Your Business
30 min	Effort Based Marketing
30 min	Money Based Marketing
25 min	Skill Based Marketing
210 min	Running Time

Finding your audience and building your business

A quick review of what we have done so far:

Section 1 - We determined that seniors are the fastest-growing segment of the population and as they transition from the work environment to retirement, they have a great need for insurance and healthcare solutions that are comprehensive and affordable.

Section 2 - We reviewed the three core products that make up the Senior Insurance Advisor portfolio and utilizing the 80% Sales Solution, identified the "vital few" 20% products. With Final Expense, Medicare products and Hospital Indemnity, you are now equipped to help the broadest cross-section of the population with the best fit solutions.

Section 3 - We evaluated the commission revenue opportunities of the Senior Insurance Advisor and understand the financial synergy created by taking a portfolio approach versus a one product solution. *Six-figure opportunities are a real possibility for the advisor that can master this section...*

Finding your audience and building your business.

This is the one area of challenge for most agents. They hear that 10,000 people a day are turning 65 but with the various rules, regulations and challenges find it difficult to locate the people that are supposed to be right in front of them. Make no mistake, marketing is tough and requires persistence and adherence to the "science of selling". As we review the possibilities for your marketing efforts, you will have to suspend judgment on what you think will work and what won't work. *These methods are working successfully for those people that work them.*

As a sales trainer and philosopher, I do believe that people have to work "authentically". Some of the methods described in this section will not be true to your personality or will have to be catered to fit who you are and your talents. <u>That is not an excuse not to do the hard work</u>. This is not a matter of *whether* you prospect but *how* you prospect. This is not a matter of *if* you have to do telemarketing, but instead, the script you use has to be an extension of you...authentic to your personality so it is natural and not robotic.

As I mentioned the science of selling, all forms of lead generation require you stick to it and refine it as you go, to improve your metrics. Doing it one day and giving up because "this doesn't work" is not true prospecting. We're going to take a look at the full spectrum of prospecting, lead generation and marketing and as the saying goes "Nothing begins until a sale is made". That means that nothing really begins until you are sitting down with the prospect who becomes a sale, who becomes a client, and eventually becomes a raving fan...Happy marketing!

Hierarchy of Lead Generation

- Let's begin by reviewing the types of lead generation available broadly to everyone. If you are new to sales, you will have to begin at the top of this pyramid and work your way down.

- As we will see in a moment, there are lead generation methods that cost effort, some that cost money and others that require skill such as repeat business and referrals.

- <u>There is no excuse for a Senior Insurance Advisor not to avail themselves of any and all of these options until their business becomes stable, scalable and sustainable.</u>

- **Don't look at this list and dismiss any of these options.** Lack of marketing dollars is a poor excuse and must be offset by tenacity and grit. If six-figure incomes were easy, there would be more than 8% of the population in America that earns it.

- Each one of these methods engages the "science of selling" and if you engage The Law Of Large Numbers and do enough of each activity it should generate a predictable return on investment.

- If you could pick which method you would predominantly spend your time pursuing which one(s) would it be? I hope you answered repeat business and referrals. They have the lowest cost (essentially free!) and have the highest close ratio. That puts a higher importance on each sale that you close because these two sources can only come from a *current client*. Make sure you put a premium on client relationships!

Effort vs. Money Based Marketing

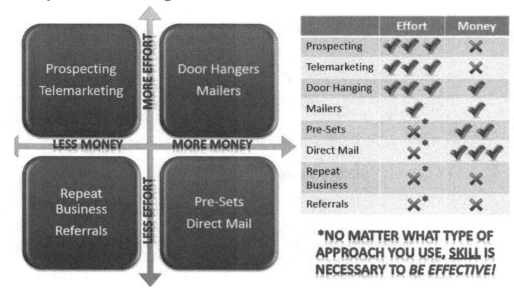

	Effort	Money
Prospecting	✔✔✔	✘
Telemarketing	✔✔✔	✘
Door Hanging	✔✔✔	✔
Mailers	✔	✔
Pre-Sets	✘*	✔✔
Direct Mail	✘*	✔✔✔
Repeat Business	✘*	✘
Referrals	✘*	✘

*NO MATTER WHAT TYPE OF APPROACH YOU USE, SKILL IS NECESSARY TO BE EFFECTIVE!

- As stated early in this program, we will assume that you are new to the business and need to build a steady pipeline of new client opportunity. If you have been successfully selling one product then you have a client base from which to build on the 80% Sales Solutions portfolio. **In order to build a business that generates six figures, you must be willing and prepared to engage all forms of marketing.**

- Of the eight methods described, two require **No Money** to engage – canvassing and telemarketing. Two methods require limited money (less than $100) – door hangers and small batch direct mail. While the cost of entry is limited with these methods, they do require more effort. As you will see momentarily, this "paying your dues phase" is the price of entry into the six-figure club.

- Two of the eight methods require a **Marketing Budget** ($1,000+ monthly) – direct mail and preset telemarketing leads. The effort of obtaining appointments is delegated to the vendor and closing the opportunities is left to the advisor.

- As clients are obtained through effort marketing and money marketing, the goal has to be repeat business and referrals.

 The most successful Senior Insurance Advisors engage all types of lead generation available and build a portfolio approach of obtaining clients with a focus on repeat business and referrals.

Effort Based Marketing

Warning: Using any of these methods for obtaining Medicare Advantage clients is a CMS violation. Engaging these methods for that purpose can lead to loss of contracts, commissions and insurance licensing. Please consult the Medicare Marketing Guidelines (MMG), if needed, to clarify.

While this training manual does not do an exhaustive review of the MMG or the particular guidelines of the various carriers and the various products, it is mindful of them. The ideas, concepts and marketing approaches outlined, should allow for business growth opportunities in a way that does not violate generally accepted marketing practices.

All of these effort strategies are for the sole purpose of securing a Final Expense opportunity. **Once an existing business relationship has been established by selling Final Expense life insurance, you can compliantly market Medicare products!**

Rest assured, in a fluid sales cycle, the clients you market final expense to, are already potential clients (or purchasers) of the other core products and it will become a natural and **compliant** extension of the activities of an ethical and educated Senior Insurance Advisor.

Misconceptions and ambiguity in interpretation of CMS marketing guidelines have created an unnecessary fear for many agents. While the guidelines were created to protect the beneficiary, it also creates an environment where professional Senior Insurance Advisors can offer compliant portfolio-based solutions to a needing population. It starts with final expense.

Obtain a List of Potential Clients

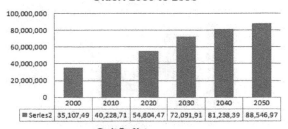

Populations Projections for People 65 and Older: 2000 to 2050

	2000	2010	2020	2030	2040	2050
▣ Series2	35,107,49	40,228,71	54,804,47	72,091,91	81,238,39	88,546,97

First	Last	Gender	Phone Number	Omit Do Not Call(DNC) registry listings	Address	City	State	ZIP	Birth Month	Birth Year
Joe	Smith	Male	(123) 474-8356		934 Sweet Bay Ct	Macon	GA	31204	6	1948
Joe	Bridges Jr	Male	(123) 474-8393	Take Note!	2906 Victoria Cir	Macon	GA	31204	6	1948
Jane	Bryant	Female	(123) 474-7818		146 Calloway Dr Apt J	Macon	GA	31204	6	1948
Julia	Childs	Female	(123) 474-8318	*DO NOT CALL*	621 Willow Creek Dr	Macon	GA	31204	6	1948
Henry	Fonda	Male	(123) 745-1140		159 Holmes Ave	Macon	GA	31204	6	1948

- Obtaining a list of people about to turn 65 or are already over 65 is the starting point. Your current agency may have access to that list (at no or very low cost to you) or you can purchase a list from a **reputable** list vendor. A search on the Internet would demonstrate that there are numerous companies who specialize in compiling these lists.

- There are two key factors in buying a list – the accuracy of the data, particularly when the list will be used for telemarketing, and up-to-date scrubbing against the Do Not Call (DNC) Registry. An inaccurate list, even for free, will not be effective, instead likely frustrating.

- The type of list you buy will also be governed by the strategy you are going to engage. If you are going to do canvassing, the list doesn't have to be as accurate, but if you are telemarketing or doing direct mail, it needs to be precise.

- Though we are targeting Final Expense as the lead-in product, we also want to set our demographic filters to include people who would be likely candidates for Medicare Products and Hospital Indemnity to round out our portfolio opportunities. The two key filters are **age and income**. Let's take a closer look at both;

  - **Age** - This demographic filter allows you to "zone in" on people aging in or turning 65. Choosing a list of people 3 to 6 months from 65 gives you a targeted audience that is transitioning from the workplace to retirement. It is a time when they are most receptive to handling matters like insurance.

o As you engage and complete the life insurance discussion, this group is also favorable for Medicare products and hospital indemnity. **Recall the Medicare Advantage commission for Initial Enrollment is higher and not prorated. Medicare supplemental will also be considered an open enrollment for this group and typically paid at full commission.**

o Also be aware that this group is heavily targeted and marketed because of these favorable selling opportunities. It is good to mix in bands of ages (such as 67-69 or 71-73) to include people who may not have as many options of choice, but who are not as heavily marketed.

o **Income -** Financial ability to purchase the various products is important but should also be viewed through the lens of the desire of consumers to have the most comprehensive coverage available at an affordable cost.

o The history of final expense is actually an evolution of the older industrial policies and more contemporarily referred to as debit insurance. It was designed to provide a low face value with affordable premiums to handle burial expenses. Because the senior population has pre-existing health conditions, it has become a matter of insurability as well as affordability. Thus final expense can be broadly marketed across a wide income spectrum. Each demographic and ZIP Code that you target should consider this.

o In Section 1, we reviewed that 39% of all Medigap policy purchasers had incomes of $20,000 to $40,000. Additionally, the data shows that an equal percentage (39%) had incomes of $10,000 to $20,000. If you were marketing final expense with an eye toward a Medicare Supplemental opportunity, you could choose a range of $15,000 to $35,000 to generate a good range of opportunity with a high likelihood of qualified prospects.

o Prospecting for final expense with an eye toward Medicare Advantage opportunity is even broader. Consider that the majority of plans are zero premium options and affordability is not a necessary consideration as it would be with Medicare Supplemental.

o Additionally, dual eligibles (Medicare and Medicaid) are historical purchasers of final expense (think back to the debit insurance statement) and they are joining Medicare Advantage plans to include D-SNPs at a rate of 20%.

o   **As with any marketing strategy, the tactics have to laser in on where you believe you can have the greatest ROI (Return on Investment) and be effective.** *Target ZIP Codes with which you are familiar but also have an eye on Medicare products – their availability and favorability.* **Do not target selling final expense in a geography where there is limited Medicare options or the options aren't attractive.**

Obtaining a list is the foundation of effort based marketing. No to low cost of entry gives you an immediate opportunity to build a client base and help you transition to other lead generation methods.

Do your homework regarding geography, and filters such as age and income. Target market your ideal audience where you feel you will have the greatest success for the effort.

Create a mix of filters with an eye on Medicare products to include Medicare Advantage and Medicare Supplemental. Test a range of age and income to find a "sweet spot".

Ask your agency if they have lists available for you to work or cost share a list with other like-minded Senior Insurance Advisors.

Pay your dues and prospect every day until you are financially able to spend money on marketing and build a base of clients.

Others have done it…so can you!

Working That List

A final reminder: All of these strategies are for the sole purpose of securing a <u>Final Expense</u> opportunity. **Once an existing business relationship has been established by selling Final Expense life insurance, you can compliantly market Medicare products.**

Canvassing   **Telemarketing**   **Door Hangers**   **Mailers**

Prospecting is a necessary activity for all salespeople but particularly Senior Insurance Advisors. Life insurance is still one of those products that people want to "put off" for a better day. Statistics demonstrate that most people purchase insurance once they have been approached. It is not top of mind until some life-changing event occurs, such as the death of a loved one, or a major illness.

The four prospecting methods listed above are **effort based marketing** approaches. Canvassing and telemarketing require <u>no money</u>, especially if you secured a list from your agency. Door hanging and small batch mailers have minimal cost of less than $100, but put you in the mix of activity. As Newton's law states,

"An object in motion stays in motion."

but conversely

"An object at rest stays at rest."

These four methods also engage a different science other than Newton's – **the law of large numbers**. Understand that for every 100 doors you knock on, 100 calls you make, 100 door hangers you place and every 100 mailers you send, there is a science that undergirds the results. If your business need a jumpstart this is the way to do it.

In order to get off of the sidelines and into the game, you've got to do the hard work of prospecting but understanding based on the first three sections of this manual, that this is a great need of the population and a great reward to Senior Insurance Advisors who pay their dues.

Canvassing

- For many agents of the 21st century, canvassing is considered a "throwback" to the days of debit insurance and vacuum cleaner salespeople. In this day of email, texting and social media many believe they are above this type of activity and have written it off as ineffective.

- Certainly, there is a negative perception of any form of "intrusive" marketing – from the perfume sprayers, the cell phone booths in the mall or the furniture salesman waiting at the front door the moment you walk in. **They are intrusive unless you need what they are marketing.**

- Prospecting is a mental exercise as much as it is a physical activity. Building up a rejection resistant mindset is not easy and normally separates those that will be successful, from those that will struggle. It is not about being oblivious, where you become abrasive or a nuisance, which is where some of the negative perception comes from. It is actually more about being sensitive to the needs of the population and the fact that many will not hear about something that can solve a problem, *unless you do these activities*.

- **The most successful people keep their mind on the objective – the goal**. The strategy then has to align with that objective - in this case, canvassing. The tactics are simply the daily things you do habitually in support of that strategy. You have to do these tactics with the mindset on the objective and stick with your purpose regardless of momentary or temporary circumstances. **Do the work!**

- Remember through the law of large numbers that not everyone needs what you have to offer in the moment that you interact with them. Your only goal out of making 100 contacts is to have;

  o The majority say "no" (and yes that is a goal!).

  o Several to say "maybe" (actual presentations).

  o A few to say "yes" (sales).

  o *Over time that would make you extremely successful!*

- Think of how you want to be treated when someone is coming into the environment of your home... specifically the porch and the front door. Your goal is to go from the porch to the kitchen table.

- **Develop an effective script for the environment.** The front porch script will be different than the telemarketing script. Direct human connection and eye to eye interactions give you the opportunity to build chemistry and credibility. The objective of this interaction is not necessarily to close a new client but to set the stage for that opportunity. The script should of course be brief and lead to the next stage of the interaction with specific options. The prospect has to feel as though they have a choice (control) but at the same time move forward if a need *is present*. Otherwise, you will get quick "no's" even though they might have interest. That will take practice and refinement on your part.

- **On the porch: Be friendly and non-threatening;**

    o Take a step back and give them a "safe zone".

    o Smile, introduce yourself and tell why you are there.

        - Hello Mr. Jones my name is Brandon Clay. Our records indicate that you are turning 65 and I am sure you are getting a lot of mail about upcoming choices ... am I right?

        - I am a licensed insurance agent in the area and wanted to stop by and personally introduce myself to make you aware of **life insurance options** available to you beyond the $255 that Social Security pays for final expenses. I can also do a review of your current insurance policies to make sure you are getting the greatest benefit available for your premiums.

        - It will only take a few minutes of your time. *Is right now a good time or Friday at 10am?*

- **Sell yourself first as a professional...*then sell the appointment*.** Some people will talk to you right on the porch, some will invite you into the kitchen table and some will actually tell you to come back on Friday at 10 AM when their spouse is home. **Remember: the only goal of this interaction is to set the stage for the next interaction.**

- **Be prepared to present them with your business card or better yet a simple brochure that outlines all of your services.** You can compliantly show that you also do Medicare products on your business card or on that brochure, as long as it adheres to CMS guidelines.

- **Most Final Expense carriers have brochures or leave behind cards.** That can demonstrate you are indeed a professional Senior Insurance Advisor and that may be the additional credibility necessary to move you to the next stage of the process.

- **Set the stage for the next interaction**. If you are not going inside today and they have not set a specific future date appointment, gain agreement for you to call them back on a particular day and time. If the list you secured includes their phone number, read that number to them and confirm it is correct. Then make a note, writing it down professionally in their presence and then, call them back on that day and time without fail.

- **Here are a few additional things about canvassing;**

    o Always be mindful of your environment - **<u>safety first!</u>**

    o If possible, use the buddy system and find another like-minded Senior Insurance Advisor to work a particular area in tandem.

    o While senior centers, high-rises and retirement communities have concentrated populations of seniors, they usually have rules against solicitation. Make contact with administrators, explain to them the value of what you do and see if they will give you formal access.

    o If you run into people who are under age and not your target demographic, ask about their parents or other loved ones who may need your help. *Every interaction is an opportunity.*

    o Set a weekly goal for the number of homes you will target and the number of days a week you will engage the activity. As you will see in the Action Plan section, if you do not already have a client base, you should be canvassing 2-3 days a week. Make a plan and stick to it!

    o **Remember your target audience.** The people who are still working will have a "harried and hurried" attention span, but those who are fully retired may have all day to talk. In either event, this may be the last generation who reads their mail, answers their phone and answers their door. *This strategy aligns with the target audience.*

    o Do not let bad interactions dissuade you. If you received 100 prequalified leads today, would you close all of them? Of course not. Canvassing is no different...rejection is a part of this profession!

Canvassing is an important and necessary tool in the arsenal of the Senior Insurance Advisor, particularly those without a client base.

Work your list with an eye on the objective of harvesting the people who need what you do. Multiplied effort will deliver you from this process into a place where you have other lead generation options at your disposal.

Telemarketing

- Telemarketing, like canvassing, is an effort based activity but does not require money. It is a necessary tool in the arsenal of all sales people but particularly Senior Insurance Advisors. It is the single fastest way to build a business, but has to be done effectively.

- Canvassing requires windshield and walking time but telemarketing is "instant". It might take two hours to canvas 30 houses, but you can make 200 dial attempts in that same time over the phone. That does not make telemarketing better than canvassing and both activities need to be engaged in, until a base of clients has been achieved.

- Telemarketing allows you to call today and have an appointment tomorrow. Because you are doing your own calling and your own selling, the prospect gets to know you throughout the process. Be true to your authentic sales nature but be memorable. That is the real key to effective telemarketing.

- The only goal with telemarketing should be to sell the appointment. Fight the urge to get into specific product discussion until you are face-to-face. Yes, there will be occasion when you will give a quote over the phone, but using that as an ongoing strategy will set you up for disappointment and failure.

- An effective script is more critical with telemarketing than canvassing, since there is no way to "read" the prospect. The script has to adhere to the AIDA marketing principles: Get **Attention**, Gain **Interest**, and Build **Desire** to get them to take the Next **Action**...an appointment.

- In various surveys, there are many reasons people do not like being telemarketed to, but the ones you can control can make a difference in how effective you will be ;

  o **Sounding scripted** - Think back to the last few calls you got (that you answered) and how annoying it was to have the person sound like they were reading a script from the computer. While that may likely be the case, practice can make you smooth and effortless in your delivery. That has to be your goal.

  o **Being rushed** - We understand that you have only a few moments to get attention and gain interest, but to speak at 100 mph is not helpful. Find a pace that allows you to be smooth, understandable and relay your core purpose for the call in 15-20 seconds or less. Carefully constructed scripts can work wonders in that time.

  o **Not gaining agreement** - In sounding scripted and being rushed, the telemarketer does not gain agreement to move forward beyond the initial 15-20 second window.

They continue to speak (or read) in a fast tone for 45 seconds or more – feels like a lifetime. When they finally take a breath to ask a question, what is the prospect's most common answer? That's right… "No". Would you rather spend 15-20 seconds gaining agreement to proceed or 45 seconds and be shut down.

- o **Not sounding professional -** While the phone is an interpersonal medium you can still convey enthusiasm and professionalism, without the presence of an attitude or being an "over-the-top" Sham Wow salesman. Your demeanor should be that of a professional, marketing valuable services. You have to be friendly, non-threatening and not "robotic" using pause and powerful inflection points to get attention and build interest.

- Here are a few examples of the first 15-20 seconds;

    - o Hello Mr. Jones, my name is Brandon Clay. I see that you are turning 65…Happy Early Birthday! I am sure you are getting a lot of mail about upcoming choices and benefits options. My call is to inform you of benefits you may qualify for beyond the $255 that Social Security pays for final expenses. Do you have 2-3 minutes to discuss this?

    - o Hello Mr. Jones, my name is Brandon Clay. Pardon the interruption, but I'm calling about important life insurance updates that you may qualify for beyond the $255 that Social Security pays for final expenses. I only need about 2 to 3 minutes to help you handle this important matter. Is now a good time?

    - o Hello Mr. Jones, my name is Brandon Clay and I am a licensed Senior Insurance Advisor. This is simply a courtesy call to introduce myself and make sure you are aware of special life insurance programs that you may qualify for. Do you have 2-3 minutes?

    - o Good morning Mr. Jones, my name is Brandon Clay and I am calling about a plan available for seniors that will cover final expenses that you may have when you or a loved one passes away. I am in your area this week and I am setting appointments to discuss these plans. Is tomorrow good for you?

    - o Good evening Mr. Jones, my name is Brandon Clay and as a Senior Insurance Advisor in the area, my job is to alert seniors about final expense benefits they may quality for beyond the $255 that Social Security pays for death benefits. I am in your neighborhood tomorrow and have 10am and 3pm available…which is best for you?

- Once you have gained agreement to proceed, you then have to set the stage for the next desired action – **the appointment**. The rest of your script can be interactive, but the only goal is to set and confirm a time to meet.

- Some professional telemarketing shops will go one additional step of qualification. That is valuable to you, the agent, when you are <u>buying</u> appointments but not when you are using your time and energy **to set** appointments.

- Using The 80% Sales Solution for Final Expense, you should have a Guaranteed Issue product that you can use, in the event the prospect does not qualify for any of the other types of insurance based on pre-existing conditions. *You only jeopardize your appointment setting ratio by asking additional health questions.*

- There will be times when the prospect shows higher levels of interest but wants you to give them a quote first. Make your first and second option a live interaction so that you can review the policy visually, and resist the urge to quote over the phone. Only on the third request should you comply. Certainly, if the rates you have are substantially better, the time would not be wasted.

- **Here are a few additional things about telemarketing;**

   o Build a script that can be delivered naturally and authentically based on your personality. Rote scripting will make you robotic and shut down your effectiveness.

   o Remember your voice is your tool, use it effectively.

   o Be prepared before making the call. Make sure you have the right name and use Mr., Mrs. or Miss as appropriate.

   o Have your script ready and stick with it, but be prepared to react in "real-time".

   o Work in an organized and clean environment – no clutter!

   o Know your products. While you are not trying to sell over the phone, you don't want to lose a strong opportunity because you are not versed in your products.

   o If possible use the buddy system and find another like-minded Senior Insurance Advisor to call with, for accountability.

   o If you run into people who are under age and not your target demographic, ask about their parents or other loved ones who may need your help. *Every interaction is an opportunity.*

   o Set a weekly goal for the number of calls you will make and the number of days a week you will engage in the activity. As we will see in the Action Plan section, if you do not already have a client base you should be telemarketing 2-3 days a week. Make a plan and stick to it!

o **Remember your target audience.** The people who are still working will have a "harried and hurried" attention span, but those who are fully retired may have all day to talk. In either event, this may be the last generation who reads their mail, answers their phone and answers their door. This strategy aligns with the target audience.

o Remember to smile and project energy and enthusiasm. Putting a mirror on your desk ensures you maintained a "sunny disposition".

o Practice... Practice... Practice.

o Evolve your process. Telemarketing requires a level of excellence which can only come from experience and refinement. Learn from every negative and positive experience.

o Trust the law of large numbers. There is a science of telemarketing that gives you a foundation of faith from which to engage it. You will develop your own metrics and eventually will have numbers you can count on such as 100 dials, 30 contacts, eight appointments and three sales. Not bad for a day's work!

Telemarketing is an important and necessary tool in the arsenal of the Senior Insurance Advisor, particularly those without a client base.

Developing an effective script and natural delivery is the key to success.

You are selling the appointment as the Desired Outcome.

The law of large numbers ensures that for focused, persistent effort, you will receive a Return on Investment.

The most successful Senior Insurance Advisors practice and refine their phone skills and make it an important part of their business development strategy.

Door hangers

- Canvassing and telemarketing require a certain "chutzpah", gumption and boldness. The profession of sales requires these three in some form or fashion. That doesn't mean we have to be aggressive to the point of being obnoxious, but we do have to have passion and purpose that gives us the fortitude we need to do the difficult things.

- The strategy of door hangers is a little less intrusive and is more of a "training wheels" approach to canvassing. It is simply a strategy of delivering direct mail by hand. By placing a colorful and informative door hanger, you create an avenue for receptive clients to reach out to you directly.

- Because it is comparable to direct mail, the return on investment will be similar. If the response rate of a strong direct mail piece is 1.5%, then you might expect 2% return on door hanging. The fact that it is on the door and not in the mailbox, gives it the greater opportunity of review. That also means that volume is the only way to generate enough activity to warrant the exercise.

- Door hangers are also a great secondary tool if the primary intent was canvassing. If you knock on a door with the intention of engaging in a conversation but no one answers, you can leave a door hanger behind.

- Most Final Expense companies offer professionally designed brochures or door hangers that you can receive at no cost or minimal cost. If you are looking to brand your business then you can produce these locally at office supply stores or printers at a reasonable cost. If you are highlighting your business, then you can showcase the range of products you offer as long as you are mindful of CMS regulations.

- If the goal is to generate direct opportunities to sell final expense, then the product should be the focus. See the following example as a guide, but understand you can now tell more of your story based on the client's interest. Your ultimate goal is still to secure an appointment.

- Most final expense companies offer a pre-need preparation guide to help people plan their funerals. These can be simple guides or they can be elaborate programs that help people leave informational legacies to future generations. Review the options available and utilize them to build interest and credibility. There is no need to reinvent the proverbial "wheel".

- Most agents are unaware of all of the tools that carriers make available as part of their marketing package. Make it a goal to review all of your carrier materials and begin utilizing them.

Our records indicate that you may be entitled to extra senior benefits. I came by to drop off your benefit package (turn over for more information).

For Re-Delivery Call:

Name: _____

Phone: _____

Please leave your name & number.

DON'T LEAVE YOUR FAMILY WITH THE BURDEN OF OUTSTANDING DEBTS FROM YOUR FINAL EXPENSES!

According to a recent survey, the average funeral now costs around **$12,500**. Many Americans still believe that the government will pay for their funeral, however, the government death benefit only pays $255 to those who qualify.

Protect your family through the new Supplemental Final Expense Program that could cover 100% of your final expenses not paid by the government. Thousands of families nationwide have already taken advantage of this program which has immediate death benefit, and pays up to **$25,000** for each person covered.

These plans are designed to help pay those expenses **NOT PAID** by government funeral plans. Currently, you may qualify even if you have a health condition.

* According to the Texas Funeral Directors Association. Not affiliated with or endorsed by the Social Security Administration

Learn how you can get this valuable protection today!

As a licensed benefit specialist I will personally provide a No-Obligation review of these and other benefits you may be entitled to. Call the number on the other side of his card and let me know which amount you require when you call:

( ) $3,000
( ) $5,000
( ) $7,000
( ) $10,000
( ) $15,000
( ) $20,000
( ) $25,000

Door hangers are essentially direct mail pieces "hand-delivered" and response rates would be comparable.

While it is a less intrusive strategy, it will require volume to generate a return and that means more effort.

It is a viable option when combined with canvassing and telemarketing in a synergistic approach.

Small Batch Mailers

- If you have some money to work with, then small batches of mail can be an effective way to get your name in front of potential clients and let them know of the services you offer.

- If vendor based direct mail is cost prohibitive ($300-$400 per 1,000), then you can do small batch Mailers on your own, 100 pieces at a time. Due to the smaller volume, you will pay first-class postage of $.49, or less if you do a postcard. The cost per 100 pieces should be about $55.

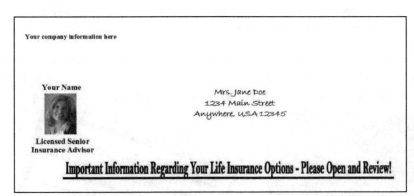

- A letter is most effective, particularly if the front address information is hand written. Yes, more time-consuming but the goal is to get a higher open rate. You can also include your photo on the front (using a good printer at home) letting them know you are a licensed Senior Insurance Advisor.

- The interior message comes next and you will either showcase your business with a letter of introduction or a specific product. If you go with a product approach, most final expense carriers have great templates that have been professionally designed for this purpose. They also have brochures you can include to build interest and credibility.

- It is most effective with a follow up telemarketing campaign referencing the letter. The combination of direct mail and the phone is powerful!

- If you have a current client base and want to introduce them to your portfolio of products then small batch direct mail will be highly effective also. It should also be followed up with a direct phone call referencing the letter and materials you sent them.

For limited cost, small batch direct mail can be a good option for lead generation, particularly if you have an existing client base to market new products.

For maximum results, a follow-up phone campaign should be conducted.

Money Based Marketing

The next strategies are money based marketing approaches. Once you have an initial revenue stream, you have to begin investing back into your business with other lead generation vehicles. Effort based marketing it is a "DIY" (Do It Yourself) approach. With money based marketing, you pay others to do it. There is a potential blessing in that your time is now freed up to pursue closings, but also a potential challenge because you are paying for something which you can't fully control the results.

As we will see at the end of this section, Monitoring, measuring and managing, will be the keys to making sure your precious marketing dollars are well spent.

There are two primary sources for money based marketing lead generation – preset appointments and direct mail response. While there is a higher cost, the combination of saving time and getting in front of more clients allows you to maximize the revenue opportunity of portfolio selling.

Pre-sets   **Direct Mail**

Preset Appointments

- **Instant Opportunity** - The value of working with a vendor to set appointments, is that you can order them today and be in the home tomorrow. The hours of telemarketing have been delegated to this vendor, thus saving you time, energy and effort.

- **Higher cost acquisition** - Of course, since you are paying for their time and effort you will have a higher acquisition cost to secure an appointment and a client. This is something you have to measure in order to ensure you have a profitable campaign.

- For example, if you are paying $25 per appointment and you order 20 appointments, that equals $500. There are several things you need to measure;

  - **Breakeven** – If the average commission is $500, then one sale is breakeven.

- o **Cost per sale** – If you close 5 sales then you would divide $500/5 = $100 per sale.

- o **Appointment rate** – If you order 20 appointments and only get to see 12 people, you have a 60% appointment rate. *The higher this number, the higher the quality of appointment that is being set.*

- o **Close rate** – If you see 12 people and close 5, you have a 42% close rate.

- o **Profitability** – If you closed 5 people and earned $3000, but you spent $500 for those leads, you have a profit opportunity (operating revenue) of $2,500. Additionally, if you sell other products besides Final Expense, then that revenue should be attributed to this campaign.

Before selecting a company to work with, there are a few things you would want to ask;

- **Are the calls recorded and how quickly you can get a copy if requested?**

  - o You should always randomly check the quality of the calls and the conversations. Even if you are getting good results, you want to know because ultimately, this vendor and the actual person making the call are representing *you*.

- **Are the appointments being set, verified by a supervisor?**

  - o To ensure that appointment quality is high, most telemarketing shops verify appointments with a supervisor. This is important so that frontline telemarketers don't set bogus appointments to meet quotas or people on the phone simply say "yes" to get them off the phone.

- **Are they asking additional qualification questions?**

  - o If you are doing your own telemarketing, additional qualification questions will lower your appointment rates. If you are paying for appointments, you want a higher level of qualification to ensure you have a higher close rate.

  - o If possible, request that the telemarketers ask basic questions such as hospitalization in the past two years, previous heart attack, stroke or cancer. These are obvious questions that would determine what type of coverage they would qualify for and while you have Guaranteed Issue in your portfolio, it should be the product of last resort.

- **Can you see a copy of the script?**

  - o Of course, as you listen to recorded calls you will know what is being said but it is good to get a script prior to establishing a relationship.

- **Do they have any performance guarantees?**

- o You should always pay for an appointment and not for the time it takes the telemarketer to set the appointment. That way your $500 guarantees you 20 appointments and not 20 hours of the telemarketer's time and therefore the potentially variable amount of appointments. Beyond this, if the appointment rate falls below a certain range (due to no shows), will they be willing to guarantee a minimum number or replace them with new appointments.

- **Can they give you references to other agents who have used their services?**

  - o Yes, you may end up talking to a "ringer" who will say nice things for a variety of reasons, but if you get two or three names and actually speak to them, you will likely be able to determine whether you want to do business with the company or not.

Working Pre-Sets

- Any lead that you sweat and work for, should have high value in your mind. When you do effort based marketing, you understand *who* is doing the work and *how* they are doing it. Conversely, any lead that you **pay** for should have even **higher value** because of the unknowns and things you can't control.

- The power of presets is that they already set the stage for you, the Senior Insurance Advisor to show up on a <u>particular day, at a particular time</u>. You will need to work them in such a fashion that "trusts the process" – but one that you will trust but verify through measuring, monitoring and managing.

- Meticulous execution - **You should never call ahead, after the appointment is set.** If the vendor has done their job, then the client is *expecting you*. Any other outreach prior to the meeting only gives them a chance to back out. You will monitor the no-show rate and appointment rate, <u>but for now, simply show up and be on time</u>.

- Have the proper mindset. Do not prejudge the lead based on any of the information included on the lead. Some companies will put little notes that can provide you with insight into the prospect, but it is your job to uncover and cultivate their needs and turn that into a sale.

Preset appointments are an excellent way to maximize your time and generate immediate opportunity.

The key to success is to monitor, measure and manage the vendor relationship to ensure a positive Return on Investment.

Turnkey Direct Mail

- Outsourcing direct mail is another powerful lead generation activity. It is one where the science of marketing is most evident and results are fairly predictable. It will be important to work with a large reputable marketing organization to ensure that economies of scale give you the best chance of success for the money you spend.

- Most lead companies require at least 1000 pieces per mail drop and costs can range from $300 to $450 per thousand, depending on the piece. Some generate call-in responses that will get routed back to you, others do BRC's (Business Reply Cards) where the prospect mails in their request to be contacted.

- Unlike preset appointments, direct mail may take several weeks before you begin to get responses. You have to take this into account based on your revenue goals and cash flow needs.

Before selecting a company to work with, there are a few things you would want to ask;

- **What is your typical response rate?**

  o While there is no easy or standard answer to this question, they should be able to provide you with guidance based on the millions of pieces that they mail.

- **What pieces have the best <u>response rates</u> and which ones have the best <u>close rates</u>?**

  o Again there is no easy or standard answer. Some mail pieces offer a free giveaway which generates a higher response rate but potentially not so well on close rate. Other pieces give the prospect a specific face amount to request and that may lower response rate but raises closing rates. They can offer you guidance based on your objectives and product strategies. Look at this example;

ATTENTION! IMPORTANT BENEFIT INFORMATION

We are pleased to announce the availability of a final expense life insurance program in **State**. Thousands of families nationwide have already taken advantage of this program which has an immediate death benefit, and pays up to **$25,000** for each person covered. These plans are designed to help pay those expenses **NOT PAID** by government funeral plans. Currently, you may qualify even if you have a health condition! To see if you qualify, mail this postage paid card **today!** You will not be charged for this information!

Check benefit requested: ( ) $3,000 ( ) $5,000 ( ) $7,000 ( ) $10,000 ( ) $15,000 ( ) $20,000 ( ) $25,000

X _Jane Doe_
SIGNATURE

Mrs. Jane Doe
123 Main Street
Everywhere, SC 12345

11
224

_67_
AGE:

_69_
SPOUSE AGE

(_123_) _555-9878_
AREA   PHONE

Please verify address. Not affiliated with or endorsed by any government program

- **How soon after receipt of a BRC do they deliver the lead?**

  o Since the lead time can be 2 to 3 weeks, you want to make sure that you receive any responses timely so you can work them quickly. To have a BRC sitting in the mail room for three days can cost you the opportunity. Many companies have online systems where you can pull down a copy of the lead.

- **Do they have an online campaign review system?**

  o Many of the large national mail houses have an online system that will allow you to review the performance of your mail campaign online and keep up with some of the critical metrics, such as response rates.

- **Do they have any performance guarantees?**

  o Ultimately, you take the risk of the performance of the direct mail campaign. However, in the event that the campaign "tanks", is the company willing to do anything to assist, such as dropping another 500 pieces.

There are several things that you can do to ensure a better rate of return and a more successful campaign;

- **Pick the right list criteria for your strategy.** While a good mail house will help you with demographic information such as age, income and ZIP Codes, you have to understand how you're going to engage the leads you receive. As we have discussed earlier, you have to market final expense with an eye on Medicare products and hospital indemnity.

- **Provide a mix of criteria to test response rates and receptivity**. Do not market any age or income exclusively. While this has a lot to do with your budget, you have to be willing to evolve your strategy if it is not working.

- **Try a mix of creative.** Creative is the actual piece that you send in the mail. If the vendor has a selection, try various pieces to see which ones pull the best and most consistently. Again, budget will govern how much variety, but be willing to test.

- **Increase response rate with 2,000 pieces per drop.** Direct mail is largely scientific and the larger the group, the more the results will adhere to industry standards. Rather than drop 1000 a week, drop 2000 every other week. Remember you are trying to increase your odds to meet or exceed anticipated response rates.

- **Conduct drops based on your monthly revenue goal.** While direct mail should not be your only lead generation source, you should delegate some percentage of your sales to this method. We will discuss objectives, strategies and tactics later, but in summary, if you need 40 leads a month from direct mail and the response rate is 1.0% then you need to drop 4,000 pieces of mail or two campaigns (2 x 2,000). You close 40% and you will get 16 sales from direct mail. Your tactics have to align with your strategy, which have to align with your revenue objectives.

- **You have to be consistent.** People who "dabble" in direct mail, starting and stopping without consistency will not have much success. While you must be willing to measure, monitor and manage the results, you have to be committed to direct mail for a portion of your lead generation.

- **You must respond immediately**. When you receive a BRC or a lead you must act quickly and effectively.

  o Using the approach from the section on telemarketing, you are calling to **set an appointment** and not trying to sell over the phone. You should reference the fact that you were calling based on their request for information and that you will be in their area in the next day or two. Set a day and time to meet with them.

  o In the event the BRC does not have a phone number, you should go directly to the home and attempt to meet the prospect. If there is no answer, you can leave your contact information.

Direct mail is a mainstay and foundational lead generation system for the largest carriers down to the independent Senior Insurance Advisor. It is a predictable and reliable way to build a pipeline of opportunity.

You must be willing to be consistent and test various creative and demographic filters until you find a model that works best for your business.

Consistency and meticulous execution on lead opportunities received is the key to making direct mail a successful strategy.

Measure, Monitor and Manage the Results

In order to make sure you reach your objectives and that the strategies are working, you have to measure, monitor and manage the tactical elements. Lead generation success is tied to the law of large numbers, so you should be able to count on a level of effectiveness – **results.** Surely those results will vary based on a number of things, but without review you will not know how to tweak and refine.

Measure - It takes time, energy and effort to conduct any type of lead generation. The stakes are raised when you are actually spending money to do marketing. The only way you will know you are effective with those precious commodities is to measure your results. How will you know which areas are bringing you the desired return if you do not know their performance? Large companies pour over their data to measure where they are successful and route money to those areas... You should do the same. Here is a list of things you need to measure for each lead generation activity as it applies, and an example for a Direct Mail Campaign;

Example Direct Mail Campaign	
Metrics	Measurement
Costs	$800
# of Pieces	2,000
Response Rate	1.1%
# of Opportunities (BRC's)	22
# of Appts	14
Appt Rate	64%
# of Sales	6
Closing Rate	43%
Gross Revenue	$2,400
Operating Revenue	$2,400 - $800 = $1,600
ROI	200%

- **Costs** - You should keep a record of all costs by campaign so that you can know your acquisition cost by activity.

- **# of pieces** - Normally associated with direct mail, this is the total number of people who will receive the mailer.

- **# Of Dials, Contacts and Appointments** – For your own telemarketing efforts, you want to understand your ratios. For example, you make 80 dials in an hour, actually speak to (contact) 12 people and set 3 appointments.

- **Response Rate** - Also, normally associated with direct mail, this is the percentage of people that respond to the activity.

- **# Of Leads/Opportunities** – If you are doing Pre-sets, this is the number of appointments scheduled. For direct mail, it would be the number of BRCs returned that still have to be converted from opportunity to appointment.

- **# Of Actual Appointments** – Conversion of opportunities to appointments.

- **Appointment Conversion** – Actual Appointments/Opportunities as a percentage.

- **# Of Sales** – How many people do you actually close/sell a product.

- **Closing Rate** – Sales/Appointments as a percentage.

- **Gross Revenue** – How much commission those sales generate.

- **Operating Revenue** – Gross revenue minus costs (all expenses of the campaign).

- **ROI** – Operating Revenue/costs as a percentage return.

Monitor & Manage - Measuring is a good start but it is only a beginning. You have to monitor the results to be sure that they are falling within acceptable ranges. If they fall out of acceptable ranges then you need to manage the campaigns and make the changes necessary to increase their effectiveness. Monitoring and Managing also ensures that you funnel most of your time, energy and money into the areas that can bring the greatest ROI.

- **For direct mail, the most critical metrics is response rate.** If it falls too low (.75% or lower) then you would need to tweak and refine the campaign. Maybe change the piece you are using, or change the age and/or income criteria.

- **For preset appointments, the most important metrics is appointment rate.** Until they are run successfully, they are still just opportunities. If you buy 20 pre-sets and have 15 no-shows, your appointment conversion doesn't likely support your investment.

- For your own telemarketing, the **# of dials, to number of contacts, to actual appointments,** all blend to determine your effectiveness.

   o If you are dialing and not making contact successfully, you may have to change the time of day for this effort. For example, when the weather is warm people will be outside from early morning to noon before it gets too hot. Calling at 9 AM may not yield great results. Changing that time to 1 PM could make all the difference.

   o If you are making sufficient contacts (reaching prospects) but not making enough appointments, then you likely need to refine your script.

Prospecting and lead generation are the lifeblood of any sales professional, but particularly the Senior Insurance Advisor.

It will take energy, effort and investment to build a sustainable lead generation program.

In order to assure effectiveness you must Measure, Monitor and Manage those results.

Skill Based Marketing

What if you could arrive at your office every day and have business waiting for you?

What if your current clients had reached out asking about other products or additional coverage?

What if their friends, family and colleagues were calling because they had been referred to you?

This should be the goal of every Senior Insurance Advisor – <u>to be so busy with repeat business and referrals that the other activities don't have to be engaged in, as predominate focus.</u>

Is that possible? Yes, but it will take time, energy and effort. It will take you passing through the Effort Phase of your business, into the Skill Phase where your expertise and organized process make it possible.

As you have seen in the previous section on effort based marketing, each sale you produce is precious and is only the beginning. You have to make that initial sale with two additional things in mind for that client:

Repeat Business with Existing Clients

Referrals

The key to both of these is what happens during the initial sale and after it. While you are focused on closing the product you are there for, you have to have your mind on future opportunity. Let's examine the various approaches based on the initial product whether it was final expense or a Medicare product.

Repeat Business with Existing Clients

If you already have an existing client base, then you have immediate opportunities to generate additional business. The approach you take with this clientele will be based on the product that you sold them initially. Because you have an Existing Business Relationship (EBR) you can do outreach for Medicare products compliantly.

For each existing client and for every new client you sell in the future, you will want to conduct a Needs Analysis. It is simply a series of questions that allows you to offer solutions that will be a best fit. Here is a high level review of that Needs Analysis;

What is your lead product?

Final Expense
- Financial Needs Analysis
- Scope of Appointment
- Medicare Advantage
- Hospital Indemnity
- Medicare Supplement

Medicare Advantage
- Financial Needs Analysis
- Hospital Indemnity
- Final Expense

Medicare Supplement
- Financial Needs Analysis
- Final Expense

Final Expense -

• You can conduct a **Needs Analysis** to determine other product opportunities.

• You have an **Existing Business Relationship** (EBR) to engage the member in a Medicare product conversation.

• You will still need **Scope of Appointment** (SOA) to conduct actual presentation at least 48 hours after sales of insurance.

• Even if client does not have an election to exercise, still obtain a SOA – *they do not have an expiration date and will allow you to go see them in the AEP (Oct 15th – Dec 7th).*

• You should schedule an **Annual Review** to make sure all insurance and healthcare choices are still the best fit and to maintain client contact.

Medicare Products -

• You can conduct an *after the sale* Needs Analysis to determine other product opportunities.

• You have to wait 48 hours to sell/market a final expense product (life insurance) and hospital indemnity.

• You should schedule an **Annual Review** to make sure all insurance and healthcare choices are the best fit and to maintain client contact.

Financial Needs Analysis Review

What do you need to know to help your client with the best fit products? You have to know what they have now. The simplest way to do that is to get them to show you the following;

- **All insurance policies** – This will allow you to do a premium comparison and determine if there is better coverage available. Be mindful of replacement laws and provisions and only move clients when there is a material betterment.

- **Medicare Card** – This will help you confirm that they have Medicare A & B.

- **Medicare Supplement Card** – This will provide company information and standardized plan type. The only other information you would need is the premium amount to determine potential cost savings of alternative coverage (such as Medicare Advantage).

- **Medicare Advantage ID Card** – This will tell you the carrier and core cost-sharing benefits (such as doctor/specialist and hospital copays) and possibly premium. It will also indicate if Part D pharmacy is covered or if it is a stand-alone MA plan

- **Part D Pharmacy Plan ID Card** – This will identify carrier, copays and premium. Additional review of drugs they take may be required to compare formulary availability of needed medications.

- **Medicaid Card** – Most states issue cards to full dual beneficiaries that have Medicare & Medicaid. Dual Special Needs Plans (D-SNPs) may enroll only certain types of Medicaid beneficiaries (such as QMB/QMB+) so the Medicaid type and number will be important for eligibility. Dual eligibles have continuous SEPs and can change plans at the first of each month with no restrictions.

- **LIS Letter** – If they qualified for Extra Help with Part D benefits, they would have received a letter from CMS. This will let you know if they have a continuous SEP to change Medicare Plans at the first of each month with no restrictions. It will also give the level of assistance they receive.

- **Other coverage** – You also want to take note of coverage from employers, military and other sources to make sure you have a full picture of what they have available.

- **Any information you receive should be treated as personal and confidential**. Since there are items that relate to health status, you also have to abide by all The Health Insurance Portability and Accountability Act (HIPAA) requirements that include handling of Private Health Information (PHI), just as you would applications for life and health insurance.

- The following is a sample form of the data you would need to help them across your entire portfolio platform.

Sample Needs Analysis – Data Review

Name		**DOB**	**Age**
Spouse Name		**DOB**	**Age**
Address			
City		**State**	**Zip Code**
Home Phone		**Cell Phone**	
Email			
Emergency Contact		**Phone**	
Beneficiary #1		**Phone**	
Beneficiary #2		**Phone**	
Beneficiary #3		**Phone**	

Current Insurance Policy Information

	Policy #1	Policy #2	Policy #3
Company			
Premium			
Face Value			
Type			
Current Cash Value			

Health Care Information

Main Insured		Spouse	
Medicare Part A	Yes No	**Medicare Part B**	Yes No
Medicare Part A	Yes No	**Medicare Part B**	Yes No

Medicare Supplement Plans			
Medicare Supplement	Yes No	Medicare Supplement	Yes No
Plan Type		Plan Type	
Premium		Premium	
Medicare Advantage Plans			
Medicare Advantage	Yes No	Medicare Advantage	Yes No
Carrier		Carrier	
Plan Name		Plan Name	
Pharmacy Coverage			
Part D Plan	Yes No	Part D Plan	Yes No
Premium		Premium	
Hospital Indemnity			
Hospital Indemnity	Yes No	Hospital Indemnity	Yes No
Carrier		Carrier	
Premium		Premium	
Medicaid or Other Assistance			
Medicaid	Yes No	Medicaid	Yes No
Type		Type	
LIS Extra Help	Yes No	LIS Extra Help	Yes No
Level		Level	

All Other Coverage			
Employer	Yes No		Yes No
Plan		Plan	
Military	Yes No	Military	Yes No
Plan		Plan	
Other	Yes No	Other	Yes No
Plan		Plan	

- Most of this information will be gathered as a natural extension of the sales process and would not be in a rapid-fire questioning session. You should be taking notes with each interaction – from the first prospecting call to the sales call and beyond. *While it looks like a volume of information, most people will only have a few of the items above.*
- The most effective way to remain compliant but also allow for a more seamless gathering of this vital information, is to **hand-deliver final expense policies** once issued. While this activity is a throwback to a day gone by, delivering a policy sets the stage for repeat business and referrals. We will discuss that more in **Section 5 – The Sales Process**.
- It will likely take 2-3 visits for you to conduct all of the business necessary to build the most comprehensive solution for your clients, but as you have seen, it is the highest benefit to all. Be patient, do not be in a hurry to oversell but make sure you have done the proper analysis before offering the best fit solutions.

Your clients are looking for the most comprehensive coverage that they can afford. They need the assistance and guidance of a Senior Insurance Advisor to walk them through the process.

It is only through evaluation of their current situation that you can offer a best fit solution… *and that requires analysis.*

As you gather information you will be able to build the proper portfolio solution. Be patient, take your time and get help when you need it.

Generating Referrals

It is no surprise that referrals are the best type of new client lead generation. What is surprising is that most people in sales do not ask for them. The core reason can be answered in one word - *relationship*.

In a transactional environment, relationships are not built. A product is needed, a product is offered and a sale is consummated, <u>but a relationship is not formed</u>. As a result, salespeople do not request referrals because deep down they know they have not earned the right to ask for them. Additionally, clients are afraid to put themselves on the line for someone they are not fully confident in.

While there are a myriad of ways to ask for and to receive referrals, the best way is to build a relationship and to become their trusted Senior Insurance Advisor. The interactions required to help a client with the comprehensive coverage they need, gives you ample opportunity to build a trusted relationship. Here are some additional strategies and tactics to generate referrals;

- **Ask for them!** As simple as that sounds, even when good relationships are formed, salespeople do not ask. If you have done a good job and sincerely implemented the best fit solution possible, then you should ask for referrals with confidence!

- **Structured follow-up**. Most salespeople consider their work done once the products are in place. The more time between interactions, the more opportunity for someone else to come in and replace your work with better solutions or for your clients to refer to other professionals – *or simply forget who you are*. If you build a structured approach to client contact then you will always be top of mind.

  - **Personal policy delivery** - As mentioned, a good time to interact with the beneficiary is when the policy has been approved and issued. While you are completing the Needs Analysis, you can have them begin thinking of other people who need this type of assistance. At the end of the session, have them provide you with the names and numbers. If the product is final expense or hospital indemnity, you can reach out to those people freely. If the product is Medicare Advantage, then they will have to refer the people directly to you and the referred client must reach out to you.

  - **Effective date outreach for Medicare Advantage** - After a member joins a Medicare Advantage plan, you cannot ask for referrals until *after* their effective date. That is also a logical time to call and make sure they received their member materials and ID card. You can help them set up the necessary physician visits and make sure their transition is smooth. During this time, you can do the additional Needs Analysis and set the stage for them referring other people to you.

o **Annual review and Needs Analysis** - For Medicare Advantage, because of changing benefits each year, you will want to conduct an annual review to make sure their current plan is still the best fit option. See Maximizing the AEP in Section 5 – The Sales Process for how to conduct these powerful reviews. It is also an impactful time to obtain referrals as the AEP (Annual Election Period) will be on everyone's mind!

o **High touch program** (4 - 6 contacts a year) - The most successful Senior Insurance Advisors make sure that they have at least 4-6 contacts with their client a year. It would be a combination of live interactions and various forms of correspondence, to include Thank You cards, Birthday cards and other important occasions such as anniversaries. It might also include a newsletter or an update on the industry and products. There are many companies that have turnkey, customizable content for the various industries, to ensure compliance, but also become an extra set of hands to help you with your high touch campaign.

o **Just Checking In Calls** - One of the simplest but most impactful calls you can make is a "just checking in" call. You can simply tell the client that they were on your mind and you simply wanted to say "hello". Yes, that call may turn into an issue or an item that needs following up on, or it may turn into uncovering a new need or getting a referral. None of those are the intent, it sincerely needs to be a check in.

o **Client Relationship Management (CRM) Programs** -There are several software programs and web-based systems that will allow you to keep up with all of the activity of staying in contact with your clients. Building your database of clients is one of the most important activities you can do. Its value comes not only in obtaining repeat business and referrals but also in reconciling commission statements from the various carriers.

Referrals are a natural extension of a trusted relationship. Providing comprehensive solutions in an atmosphere of excellence in service is the surest way to build raving fans who will refer you to everyone they can.

Senior Insurance Advisors who stay in contact and meet the ever-changing needs of their clients will never want for business opportunities.

Section 4 Summary

Section Four Summary

- Nothing begins until you are in front of a prospective client and a sale is made.

- Lead generation is a vital part of the sales profession and each Senior Insurance Advisor must be ready and willing to engage in business development.

- There is Effort-Based, Money-Based and Skill-Based marketing strategies that are available to build a sustainable business. Each one must be utilized and blended to build a stable, scalable and sustainable revenue model.

- Obtaining a list of potential clients for canvassing, telemarketing, door-hanging and direct mailing for the purpose of selling Final Expense, should be the foundation of all new Senior Insurance Advisors.

- Once cash flow allows, Pre-set appointments and large scale Direct Mail should be engaged by all advisors.

- All forms of marketing campaigns should be Measured, Monitored and Managed to provide the highest ROI and ensure effective use of time, energy and money.

- Leverage the available tools from your agency partners and the carriers to present the most professional image possible and tap into existing programs for economies of scale.

- Repeat Business and Referrals are the highest quality opportunity, with the highest close rate potential.

- Conduct full Needs Analysis as a way to create Repeat Business with existing clients, using your portfolio of products for the best fit solution.

- Building a quality relationship is the key to obtaining Repeat Business and Referrals, and a structured High Touch Program is the best practice for that outcome.

End of Section Four

SECTION NOTES

_____

_____

_____

_____

_____

_____

_____

_____

_____

_____

_____

_____

_____

_____

_____

_____

_____

_____

SECTION NOTES

SECTION NOTES

Section 5: The Sales Process

 Time Required: 1 Hour 30 Minutes

Time Remaining: 1 hours 00 minutes

What you will learn in this session;

20 min	Final Expense
10 min	Medicare Supplement
10 min	Hospital Indemnity
20 min	Medicare Advantage
15 Min	Maximizing the AEP
300 min	Running Time

At the kitchen table

As you are sitting down at the kitchen table drinking a glass of water so graciously offered, and having begun building rapport that is a natural extension of human connection, you can calm your mind based on *one thing – **you have already done the most difficult part!***

The success of your lead generation efforts have brought you here, with an opportunity to help someone solve a problem or meet a need. That is an awesome opportunity and privilege!

While this manual will provide you with a roadmap for conducting presentations, **rote scripting is not the intention**. You must be able to operate within the framework of your "authentic sales voice". That is the only voice that is sustainable, natural and can lead to your success. The senior population, while less skeptical than their younger counterparts, *are very intuitive*. Many are able to sense right away that you are out of character.

There is no need for undue pressure or strong-arm tactics. The need for the portfolio of products already exists, now you need to determine the best fit solutions and advise them in an ethical manner. Certainly, you will not close 100% of the people you see at the kitchen table but if you keep their best interest front of mind, you will be successful.

Many carriers provide presentations for you to use in order to assist you in delivering your message. In fact, most Medicare Advantage companies require that you use provided flipbooks or presentation manuals to ensure compliance, beneficiary understanding and best fit product selection. Before you go to the home, you should always do call planning to make sure you have everything you need;

- Presentations for the key products or supporting brochures and information.

- Rate charts (in print), smart phone/tablet apps, or computer. Be prepared just in case there is a technical issue.

- The proper applications for the products you represent or have predetermined would be a best fit solution.

- Key phone numbers to the carrier's home offices and/or verification services for life applications.

- Blank Needs Analysis worksheets to fill in as you determine information.

- A supply of business cards as referral opportunities present themselves.

- Put your cell phone on vibrate and put it away – *there is nothing more important than your client!*

Final Expense Presentation

Using The 80% Sales Solution you should have 3-5 Final Expense Carriers. Don't have too much paperwork or brochures out until product selection and application time. Keep your presentation short and to the point. Don't bore, overwhelm or over sell the client. Core elements;

Opening

> *"Mr. Jones, thanks for giving me a few minutes of your time. Have you ever heard of Final Expense Insurance? Do you currently have that type of coverage?"*

Initial Review - If yes, then determine who they have it with.

> *"Mr. Jones do you know what your premium is or do you mind getting that policy so I can see if I represent a company that can increase your coverage or lower your premium?"*

If no coverage, then begin Building Need

> *"I know some of this will be uncomfortable to discuss, but is very important to assure your loved ones are protected. When you pass away, who would be responsible to pay for your funeral and other final expenses?*
>
> *Your wife Maggie?"*

Write the name on your paper so that he can see it.

Next statement

> *"Again, this may be uncomfortable, but have you ever been involved with the passing of a loved one?*
>
> *You may be aware that the average funeral today costs between $8,000 and $12,000."*

Write the amounts on your paper so that he can see it.

Next statement

> *"Will Mrs. Maggie be in a position to pay for that out-of-pocket when the time comes?*
>
> *And if you did have that cash would you want to take that amount to spend on a funeral or leave it for your wife to do other things?"*

**Payoff statement &
Initial close**

> *"Before I leave here today I can make sure that Mrs. Maggie is taken care of and when you pass she doesn't have to worry about anything.*
>
> *The senior benefit package I will provide you, will take care of it all. Isn't that the kind of peace of mind you need?"*

Allow the client to answer…

As you gain agreement it is time to transition to the products

> *As a benefit specialist, I am licensed to represent several companies and will help you choose the best coverage possible.*
>
> *In order to do that, I need to ask some questions about your health.*
>
> *Don't worry, regardless of your answers, I am sure I have a company that can provide the coverage you need.*

- Ask health questions to see what they qualify for based on the carriers you represent.

  – Standard issue/Graded/Modified

- Once you know the best product they qualify for, pick a "starting point";

  – Pick a premium or face value based on responses to your their expressed need for insurance, or the average cost of funeral and final expenses ($10k to $15k).

- Once you establish the company with best product/rate, take out that application and remove all other paperwork (eliminate distractions).

- Begin to fill in the application asking all questions relative to the carrier.

- After completed, let them know all that is needed to begin coverage is a check made out to the XYZ insurance company.

- Ask for the check!

- ***Once the application is complete, you have a client!***

- Now use the Needs Analysis to let them know you can help them in other areas.

- While you cannot do a Medicare Advantage enrollment in the same appointment you can start setting the stage.

- Let them know that you will **hand-deliver the policy once approved and issued**. At that time, let them know you will be able to review other insurance and healthcare options. In order to do so, you need to fill out a **Scope of Appointment.**

Wrap up

- **_Thank them_** for taking the time to sit down with you to complete an important item that many people procrastinate on.

- **_Congratulate them_** on taking care of such a significant part of their financial situation.

- **_Reinforce the peace of mind_** they now have being able to help their loved ones.

- **_ASK for referrals -_** anyone that they may know that would benefit from the same plan.

Final Expense can be an emotional sale due to the subject matter of death and leaving loved ones behind.

Sensitivity is key, but engaging the discussion in such a manner that the client not only sees the need, but acts on filling that need is the role of the Senior Insurance Advisor.

There is great peace of mind for the clients that handle this important piece of business and you should focus your core business in helping as many people as possible.

Medigap - The Right Choice

- As you work through the options of healthcare for the Medicare beneficiary, the conversation must include the Medicare Supplement option, also referred to as Medigap.

- Recalling the statistics from Section 1, the income ranges of people who purchase these policies are much wider than most agents realize so you should offer Medicare Supplement options to all of your clients. In your prospecting activities, you likely assessed the clients financial ability to afford a supplement and once that is established, standardization makes plan selection "simple".

- Affordability aside, one of the main selling points of these policies is the freedom of provider access. Unlike HMOs or PPOs with Medicare Advantage, where the network is restricted by contract, Medigap policies allow beneficiaries to go to essentially *any provider*. Additionally, no referrals are necessary. In areas where Medicare Advantage has poor networks or the options are not plentiful, the majority of people choose supplements.

- Medicare Supplements are standardized and provide a fixed benefit structure year over year while Medicare Advantage typically changes each year. While benefit structures are stable, annual premiums can, and typically do, rise each year. A Part D pharmacy plan must also be added to a supplement.

- **Because of standardization, the sales process for Medigap policies is somewhat "simpler". Once you determine you have a client for a Medigap policy you only need to determine which plan and which carrier – which is likely a derivation of premium, company reputation (rating) and information on annual increases.**

- While there are other factors such as open enrollment, guaranteed issue and trial periods, if the Senior Insurance Advisor focuses purely on Plan F, they will be offering the most comprehensive coverage to meet the needs of the vast majority of beneficiaries.

  o Plan F is first dollar coverage. It covers the Part B deductible, the potential Excess Charges, and offers foreign travel.

  o It covers all other cost shares after Medicare pays its part.

  o The Senior Insurance Advisor needs to make sure they are contracted with good companies that offer competitive rates.

 Once financial ability and desire to purchase a Medigap policy are known, the process is "simple" – *find a carrier that has the plan desired at a rate that can be afforded.* Sales skill is still required, but more focus will be on education and plan/carrier section.

Hospital Indemnity

As we determined in Section 2, the power of hospital indemnity is best seen when added to Original Medicare (alone) or preferably, a Medicare Advantage plan. The benefit of these plans has been reviewed, so the next step is to know when to engage the product in the portfolio discussion. There are several logical times;

- **During the Financial Needs Analysis when you are asking about existing indemnity coverage.** If they do not have a policy, then you can explain what it is and how it works.

- **Ask if they have ever been hospitalized or if they understood how it would work with their current coverage if a hospital stay was needed.**

  - If they have had a hospitalization, make sure they understand how those costs would work with Original Medicare or the Medicare Advantage plan they are on or reviewing.

  - Writing those figures on paper so they can see the impact is most powerful.

- **When you are delivering an approved Medicare Advantage presentation, you can mention indemnity when you discuss the inpatient copays.** While you can't sell the product at the same time as Medicare Advantage, you can establish a "placeholder" conversation to refer back to at the end of the meeting…**setting the stage for going back 48 hours later.**

- **Review the application for the desired carrier and make sure the beneficiary meets any underwriting requirements.** If they have been hospitalized recently and do not qualify, make sure you check in with them before their time period runs out. You can create a tickler file of these clients to get them a policy as soon as they qualify.

Hospital Indemnity is a product that "sells itself" when properly understood and positioned in the sales process.

For Medicare beneficiaries, hospitalization is not a matter of if…*but when.*

They want the most comprehensive coverage they can afford and hospital indemnity premiums are generally affordable based on benefit design flexibility.

Medicare Advantage

It Begins With the Right Choice

The real job of the Senior Insurance Advisor when discussing Medicare Advantage with the beneficiary, is helping them make the right choice. In order to do that, we will use a decision tree approach and then a **Coverage Review Reference Guide*** which will help the advisor sift through the various options to identify the one or two plans which would be suitable. If you are new to Medicare Advantage, *don't be overwhelmed*, these steps will become clearer as you certify with the various carriers and complete certification, such as AHIP (American Health Insurance Plans). Let's take a look at the four steps in the process.

Step One: *Determine the county the client lives in.*

Step Two: *Determine the client status*

- Full Dual – Medicare and Medicaid
- Chronic (17 Qualifying Diseases)
- Non-Dual and Non-Chronic

Step Three: *Select the best plan using a **Coverage Review Reference Guide*** which gives high level overviews of key items;*

- Premium affordability
- Co-pay structure based on their individual utilization pattern
- Network access (are key doctors in the plan or are they willing to access network providers)
- Pharmacy Formulary review
- Other important plan factors

Once a best fit plan has been selected, begin using the selected carrier's CMS approved presentation to guide the beneficiary through the plan.

Step Four: *Complete the Application!*

* The Coverage Review Reference Guide is Senior Insurance Advisor developed reference tool that is designed to assist the agent in finding the best plan for a beneficiary. It is not for beneficiary use and cannot be shown to beneficiary under any circumstance!

The Medicare Advantage Decision Tree

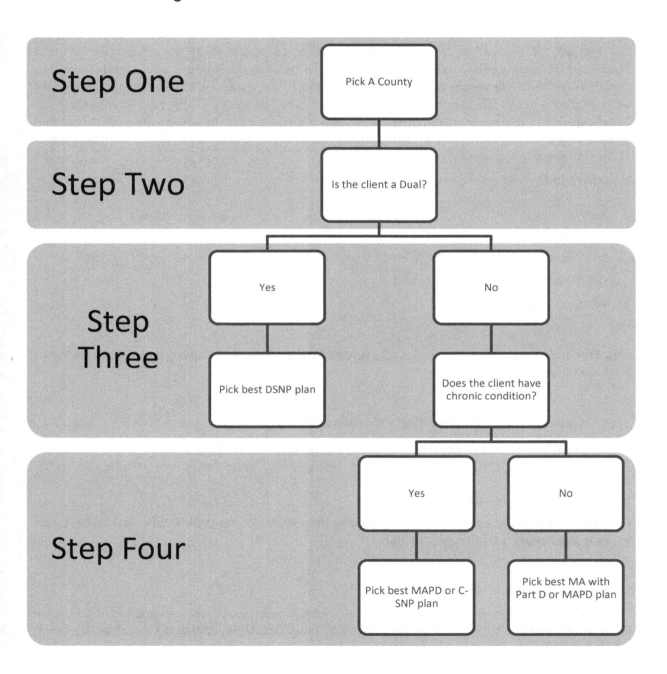

Coverage Review Reference Guide

The next series of charts will be the Coverage Review Reference Guide that was referenced above. Some FMO/agencies provide some version of these "at a glance" charts to help their agents quickly review the options available in a particular geography. If it is not provided, or the information is not available in another format, the Senior Insurance Advisor can develop this valuable resource on their own.

Admittedly, the task is tedious but the reward of this tool can have a tremendous impact on your Annual Election Period (AEP) and will be well worth it. As you examine what is contained in each chart you will begin to see its value. Luckily, you will only have to create these charts for the counties that you work in!

One last time: These charts are not for beneficiary use, distribution or to be shown to them in a home presentation!

The first chart is **Products by Carrier – Act a Glance**

	Plan A MAPD HMO-POS	Plan A MAPD HMO	Plan A MAPD HMO	Plan A MAPD LPPO	Plan A MAPD LPPO	Plan A MAPD LPPO	Plan A MAPD RPPO
Plan Type	HMO-POS	HMO	HMO	LPPO In/OON	LPPO	LPPO In/OON	RPPO
Premium	$0.00	$0.00	$0.00	$39.00	$40	$56.00	$77.00
PCP/Specialist	$15/$40 In 30%/30 OON	$10/$45	$17/$45	$15/$45 In 30%/30% OON	$15 In 30% OON	$15/$45 In 40%/40% OON	$20/$45
Inpatient Hospital	$250 days 1-7 30% per admit OON	$250 days 1-7	$260 days 1-7	$250.00 days 1-7 30% OON per admit	$260 days 1-7 30% OON Admit	$260.00 days 1-7 40% OON per admit	$260 days 1-7
OOP Maximum	$5,900	$5,900	$6,700	$6,700/$10,000	$5,500/$7,500	$6,700/$10,000	$6,700
Medical Deductible	$0.00	$0.00	$0.00	$0.00 In $500 OON	$500 OON	$0.00 In $500 OON	$0.00
Rx Deductible	$0.00	$200	$200 Tier 1,2,3 exempt	$0.00	$0	$0.00	$150
Rx Copay (T1/T2/T3/T4/T5)	$6/$15/$45 /$95/33%	$6/$15/$45/ $95/27%	$6/$18/$45 /$95/27%	$6/$18/$45/ $95/33%	$6/$15/$45/$95/ 33%	$6/$18/$45/ $95/33%	$4/$12/$45 /$95/29%

- This chart represents **one carrier only** and the various products they offer in the counties you decide to include.

- You can quickly determine plan type (normally a network designation), premium, primary care/specialist co-pay, hospital co-pay, MOOP, medical deductible if any, and a summary of pharmacy benefits.

- This puts the core benefits of one carrier in one place and not several Summary of Benefits.

The next chart is **Carrier Products Comparison by Category – At a Glance**

	MAPD Non-Chronic									
	Plan A MAPD HMO-POS	Plan A MAPD HMO	Plan A MAPD HMO	Plan A MAPD LPPO	Plan A MAPD LPPO	Plan A MAPD LPPO	Plan A MAPD RPPO	Plan B LPPO MAPD	Plan B RPPO MAPD	Plan C HMO
Plan Type	HMO-POS	HMO	HMO	LPPO In/OON	LPPO	LPPO In/OON	RPPO	Local PPO Not SNP	Regional PPO Not SNP	HMO
Premium	$0.00	$0.00	$0.00	$39.00	$40	$56.00	$77.00	$0.00	$0.00	$0.00
PCP/Specialist	$15/$40 In 30%/30 OON	$10/$45	$17/$45	$15/$45 In 30%/30% OON	$15 In 30% OON	$15/$45 In 40%/40% OON	$20/$45	$30/$50	$30/$50	$5/$35
Inpatient Hospital	$250 days 1-7 30% per admit OON	$250 days 1-7	$260 days 1-7	$250.00 days 1-7 30% OON per admit	$260 days 1-7 30% OON Admit	$260.00 days 1-7 40% OON per admit	$260 days 1-7	$419.00 days 1-4	$395.00 days 1-4	$225.00 days 1-4
OOP Maximum	$5,900	$5,900	$6,700	$6,700/$10,000	$5,500/$7,500	$6,700/$10,000	$6,700	$6,700	$6,700	$4,900
Medical Deductible	$0.00	$0.00	$0.00	$0.00 In $500 OON	$500 OON	$0.00 In $500 OON	$0.00	$0.00	$0.00	$0.00
Rx Deductible	$0.00	$200 Tier 1,2,3 exempt	$200	$0.00	$0	$0.00	$150	$0.00	$0.00	$0.00
Rx Copay (T1/T2/T3/T4/T5)	$6/$15/$45/$95/33%	$6/$15/$45/$95/27%	$6/$18/$45/$95/27%	$6/$18/$45/$95/33%	$6/$15/$45/$95/33%	$6/$18/$45/$95/33%	$4/$12/$45/$95/29%	$5/$10/$25%/25%/33%	$5/$10/$45/$95/$33%	$6/$15/$45/$95/33%

- This chart does the same thing for **<u>every carrier</u>** you represent (or competitors that you want to review).

- You can immediately compare **Plan A HMO** to **Plan C HMO**. *What is the difference in premium? The difference in hospitalization?* The core benefit design is all here.

- You should create three different charts using this methodology

  o MA PD

  o Chronic Illness Special Needs Plans (C-SNPs)

  o Dual Special Needs Plans (D-SNPs)

The next chart is **Products Available by County Grid – At a Glance**

County	Plan A LPPO	Plan A MAPD HMO	Plan A MAPD HMO	Plan A MAPD HMO	Plan A MAPD LPPO	Plan A MAPD LPPO	Plan A MAPD RPPO	Plan B LPPO MAPD	Plan B RPPO MAPD	Plan B RPPO MAPD	Plan B RPPO C-SNP	Plan B RPPO CSNP	Plan B RPPO DSNP	Plan C	Plan D HMO DSNP
A						√	√	√	√	√	√	√	√		√
B								√	√	√	√	√	√	√	
C			√	√				√	√	√	√	√	√		
D		√				√		√	√	√	√	√	√		√
E								√	√	√	√	√	√		
F								√	√	√	√	√	√	√	
G								√	√	√	√	√	√		
H				√	√			√	√	√	√	√	√		√
I								√	√	√	√	√	√		
J			√	√				√	√	√	√	√	√		√
K		√				√		√	√	√	√	√	√	√	
L								√	√	√	√	√	√	√	
M								√	√	√	√	√	√		
N								√	√	√	√	√	√		
O			√	√				√	√	√	√	√	√		

- This simple chart highlights which plans are in each county. With the exception of Regional Preferred Provider Organizations (RPPOs), most plans are available on a county by county basis.
- Focus on the counties that you will predominantly work in and simply list all of the plans available on a county by county basis.

The next chart is **Products Comparison by County – At a Glance**

County A Grid

	MAPD Non-Chronic						MAPD Special Needs Plans C-SNP			MAPD Special Needs Plans D-SNP	
	Plan A MAPD HMO-POS	Plan A MAPD HMO	Plan A MAPD PFFS-Full	Plan A MAPD RPPO	Plan B LPPO MAPD	Plan B RPPO MAPD	Plan B LPPO C-SNP	Plan B RPPO C-SNP	Plan B RPPO CSNP	Plan B RPPO DSNP	Plan D DSNP
Plan Type	HMO-POS	HMO	PFFS Full Plans	RPPO	Local PPO Not SNP	Regional PPO Not SNP	Local PPO Chronic (CSNP)	Regional PPO Chronic (CSNP)	Regional PPO Chronic (CSNP)	Regional PPO Dual (DSNP)	HMO DSNP
Premium	$0.00	$0.00	$75.00	$77.00	$0.00	$0.00	$0.00	$0.00	$14.60	$31.50	$0.00
PCP/Specialist	$15/$40 In 30%/30 OON	$17/$45	$15/$40	$20/$45	$30/$50	$30/$50	$35/$50	$25/$50	20%/20%	20%/20%	20%
Inpatient Hospital	$250 days 1-7 30% per admit OON	$260 days 1-7	$260 days 1-7	$260 days 1-7	$419.00 days 1-4	$395.00 days 1-4	$335.00 days 1-5	$335.00 days 1-5	FFS	FFS	FFS
OOP Maximum	$5,900	$6,700	$6,700	$6,700	$6,700	$6,700	$5,900	$6,700	$6,700	$6,700	$3,400
Medical Deductible	$0.00	$0.00	0.00	$0.00	$0.00	$0.00	$0.00	$0.00	$151 Combined	$151 Combined	$151.00
Rx Deductible	$0.00	$200	$0.00	$150	$0.00	$0.00	$0.00	$0.00	$310	$310	$0.00
Rx Copay (T1/T2/T3/T4/T5)	$6/$15/$45/$95/33%	$6/$18/$45/$95/27%	$6/$15/$45/$95/33%	$4/$12/$45/$95/29%	$5/$10/$25/25%/33%	$5/$10/$45/$95/$33%	$4/$9/$45/$95/33%	$4/$9/$45/$95/33%	$4/$9/$45/$95/33%	$4/$9/$45/$95/33%	Generic - $0/$1.20/$2.55 Brand - $0/$3.60/$6.35

- This is the most impactful chart because it includes all the plan options (MAPD, C-SNP and D-SNP) for a county...at a glance. If there were only one chart you were going to create, this would be the one.

- The grouping of plans will allow you to see the core benefits in an "apples to apples" comparison.

- This is not designed to be a substitute for a full review of the Summary of Benefits, but will help you use the decision tree process to get down to the "vital few" and begin building a more detailed recommendation.

- Once you have narrowed the choices down, begin utilizing the carrier supplied, CMS approved presentations.

- This Coverage Review Reference Guide is even more valuable in a pre-call in environment so that you will have narrowed down the choices prior to meeting with the client. Again, make sure you comply with all CMS marketing guidelines!

The effort expended to create a Coverage Review Reference Guide will reap great benefits to the Senior Insurance Advisor, particularly, those new to the business or Medicare Advantage products.

When utilized with the decision tree approach, it makes narrowing down plan options to the "vital few" a much easier and accurate process.

Remember: the Coverage Guide is not designed for beneficiary use and cannot be shown to them as part of a compliant presentation.

Maximizing the AEP

The 1st Challenge – Time & Money

Having enough time to help all your Current Clients...

...While finding New Ones!

Everyone is after your clients:

- They will receive their Annual Notification of Change (ANOC) from carrier.

- They will likely receive telephonic outreach from current carrier to retain member.

- They will receive mail and other outreach from carriers and agents who want to move them to a "better" product.

- You have to be educated on the options, so you can preserve them in current plan or move them to a better plan.

The 2nd Challenge – Finding Opportunity in Chaos!

The AEP is filled with various activity:

- Annual Certification

- Carrier training

- Continuing Education for licensing

- Selling current products to keep revenue coming in

- Member outreach to ensure you don't lose clients

- Trying to find new ones

- Adding the portfolio of products

The 3rd Challenge – Orchestrating and Organizing the AEP

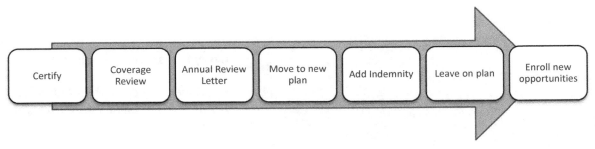

Certify | Coverage Review | Annual Review Letter | Move to new plan | Add Indemnity | Leave on plan | Enroll new opportunities

- First things first – "Don't whine and cry…certify!"

  o Do AHIP certification **the moment it becomes available**. It will help you get through most other carrier certifications quickly with less time involved.

  o Complete carrier's certifications and live trainings as soon as you can.

  o Do not procrastinate – It all means nothing if you are not appointed to sell!

- After certifications you have to organize and review your client base and book of business, specifically, Medicare Advantage clients.

  o Do you have your clients in an Excel spreadsheet or other program so you can conduct Annual Review Mailer using technology, such as mail merges?

  o If not, you need to get your clients organized for outreach.

- Complete Coverage Review Reference Guide as outlined earlier in this section so that you can have "at a glance" information available.

  o The Coverage Review Reference Guide will help you determine the best client strategy – leave on current plan or switch to better plan.

- Annual Review Mailer – This is designed to go to your Medicare Advantage clients as they are receiving their Annual Notification of Change (ANOC) letters from their current carrier. This mailer will set the stage for you as their Trusted Advisor and the person they should consult *before* they make any decision. The elements of the mailer with samples to follow;

  o Annual Review Letter. It is generic and cannot mention specific benefits.

From The Desk Of
Brandon Clay

Important information regarding your annual Medicare options:

Mr. John Smith
1234 Main Street
Anywhere, USA 98765

Dear Mr. Smith,

Yes, it is that time again! **The Annual Election Period (AEP) begins on October 15 and ends on December 7 of this year.**

As my client, I am honored that you entrusted me to help you make some of your life & health insurance decisions and I want to continue to help you make the best choice for your insurance needs. This is an important time and you will likely receive many communications regarding the upcoming Annual Election Period.

I will reach out to you to explain any coverage changes, answer any questions you may have, and if necessary, meet with you again to discuss your options. I have enclosed a **Scope of Appointment** form that is required to allow me to meet with you.

Again, I thank you for the opportunity to serve all your insurance and health care needs.

Sincerely,

Brandon Clay

Brandon Clay
Phone: 555-999-1234
License # AGR912837
I am in independent agent/broker and not affiliated with government agency.

o   Customized envelope with your picture on outside to increase open rate

**Your Logo and
Information Here!**

Your Clients Here!

**Important Information From
Your Insurance Advisor**

Your picture and name here!

John Doe

Information Regarding Your Annual Healthcare Decisions - Please Open and Review!

o   Scope of Appointment if you don't already have one on file from recent interactions (the SOA has no expiration date)

The Senior Insurance Advisor has to balance all of the necessary things to be prepared for the AEP, along with day to day activities.

In this chaotic time of year, procrastination is the single greatest enemy…lack of organization would b the second.

The Annual Review Letter is the cornerstone to running an organized AEP and is the foundation of business preservation and new business opportunities.

Staging an Organized AEP!

Stage # 1

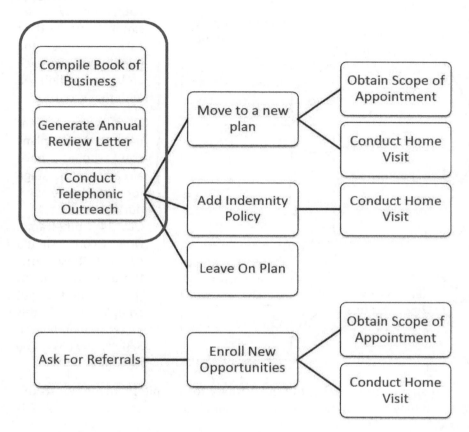

- Organize and compile your book of business and prepare Annual Review Letter. You should target your letter being received about October 1st.

- Using the Coverage Review Reference Guide you created, you should have a general idea of the changes your clients are facing from their current carrier and if they should stay with plan or switch.

- Conduct your telephonic outreach to these clients beginning October 1st and completing by October 14th. While you cannot take an enrollment during this time, you can do full presentations (CMS approved by carrier) during this time. The beneficiary can mail the application but you may not assist. This period is the best time to do your preservation activities and set the stage for those that need to move, so you can focus October 15th to December 7th , on new opportunities.

Stage # 2

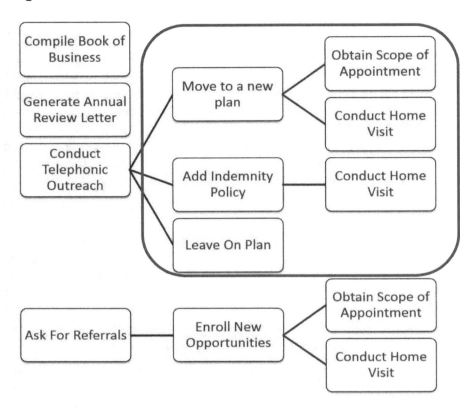

- Determine which of your clients you can simply leave on their current plan, do the telephonic outreach and you are finished with that group!

- For members that need to switch plans you should have already set the stage for the home visit during the Oct 1st – Oct 14th timeframe. Now you should conduct those visits the first two week of the AEP and target completion of this group (depending on activity required) by November 1st.

- All along the way, you should be inserting the opportunity for Hospital Indemnity. As the ANOC they just received may have an increase in the hospitalization cost-sharing, the AEP is a good time to review.

- Yes, you should market and sell hospital indemnity during this season, to existing clients and new ones. It means two visits, but the activity generated will help you build additional momentum. Never turn away a sales opportunity!

Stage #3

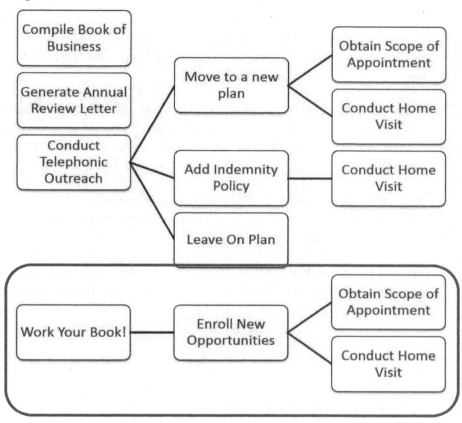

• The next 5-6 weeks of the AEP should be spent focusing on new clients, particularly, for Medicare products.

• If your client base has final expense only you can outreach to them directly since you have an Existing Business Relationship (EBR).

• Even though you may not be the agent of record, you should still conduct outreach. If they have a Medicare agent that maintains a relationship, then you should honor that professionally and not pursue. If they have not heard from their agent (common challenge of the industry) then you should provide that service.

•   For clients that you have sold previous Medicare Advantage plans to (past their effective date) you should ask for them to have any referrals they can think of, reach out to you. The prospective clients still have to call you...even during the AEP!

•   For clients that you have sold Final Expense, they may freely give referrals for you to call, if the purpose of that call is to sell life insurance. Again, do not turn down any opportunity and you should still see your focus as a Senior Insurance Advisor...not a one product agent...yes, even during the AEP.

•   For advisors that have extremely large books, then you will have to hire an assistant or temporary help to assist with the administrative elements while you focus on the revenue generating activities of your business.

The Medicare options available are many and require the Senior Insurance Advisor to be organized and logical in their approach to the business.

The best fit product selection is key to helping your clients, and use of the decision tree approach and the Coverage Review Reference Guide are vital in the process.

The AEP particularly, requires organization to execute a strategy that is focused on client preservation and new client acquisition.

Staging the AEP is the best way to leverage the opportunities created in this concentrated period of time.

Section 5 Summary

Section Five Summary

- Once you have made it to the kitchen table, you have done the most difficult part. Likely, need has already been established and your job now it to lead and guide your client through the maze of options.

- Make sure you are prepared for each sales call and do the necessary pre-call planning.

- For all products, but particularly final expense, work on developing a script that exposes need and positions your solutions properly.

- Medicare Supplements are largely driven by cost since plans are standardized. Use Plan F as your focus plan and have at least 3 carriers to provide competitive quotes.

- Hospital Indemnity should be introduced initially during the Medicare Advantage conversation when hospitalization coverage is discussed. Come back to it in the close, setting the stage for the next visit.

- Potentially complex Medicare Advantage choices are made simple with the use of the decision tree approach and use of a Coverage Review Reference Guide.

- Once a product decision has been narrowed down, most Medicare Advantage carriers have CMS approved presentations that provide effective delivery of sales material.

- The AEP is the most opportunity filled time of year, but also the most challenging. The key to success is to be organized and focused in your activities.

- Complete all certifications and carrier requirements as soon as they are available.

- Stage your AEP in order to maximize your time and energy, while leveraging your client base and new opportunities.

End of Section 5

SECTION NOTES

SECTION NOTES

SECTION NOTES

Section 6: Zero to 100k in 12-18 Months Action Plan

Time Required: 1 Hour Minutes

Time Remaining: 00 Minutes

What you will learn in this session;

10 min	The Target & The Tactics
5 min	Sample Action Plan
45	Planning for Six-Figures
360 min	Running Time

The Target and the Tactics

You now have all the tools you need to be a successful Senior Insurance Advisor. **Now all that is left is to do it!** In this final section, you will develop an Action Plan for the next 12 months with one objective – *Build a six-figure income while providing value to a deserving senior population.*

You can set whatever target you like but you must set an objective:

"If you don't know where you are going, you will probably end up somewhere else." Lawrence J. Peter

Two Things Will Determine If You Hit Your Established Targets...

1. ***How good is your aim?***

2. ***How good is your weapon?***

Once the objective is established, *the strategy is the aim and the tactics are your weapons.* You have to determine that everything you need is in place to have a real opportunity to meet your goals;

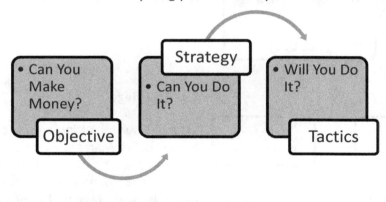

We have already determined that the Objective of a Six-Figure income is possible and we have done a deep review of strategy...then the only question that remains is tactics...*will you do what is necessary?*

Your Objectives, Strategies and Tactics must line up for you to achieve your goal and we will begin developing specific tactical approaches to make sure we will hit our target!

Building A Tactical Approach

Let's take a very high level example to illustrate how to build strategies and tactics to support your objectives. In this example, we are targeting $100,000 in revenue.

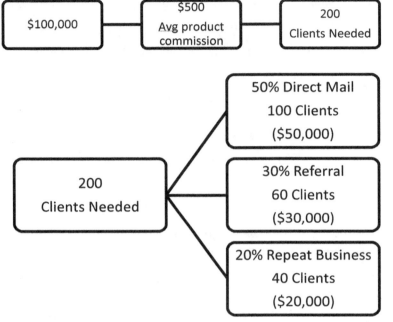

We assume a blended commission opportunity of $500 per product. The simple math 100,000/500 = 200 clients

Tier 1 Strategy

The next step is to break down our expected mix of clients. We will build our strategy around getting 50% of our clients from direct mail (one lead generation method for simplicity of example), 30% will come from referrals and the 20% will be repeat business from other products.

Tier 2 Strategy

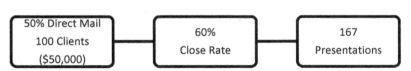

Let's put our initial focus on the Money Based Marketing that will generate the first 100 clients that will be the foundation of our referrals and repeat business opportunities. Now we have to begin making projections about various metrics of the performance of the strategy. In this example, we assume we will close 60% of the appointments we run. That informs how many "kitchen table" presentations we have to conduct;

100/.60 = 167 Presentations

Tier 3 Strategy

167 Presentations	40% Lead to Appt Rate	418 Lead	1% RR 41,800 mail peices

In the next layer of strategy, we have to make more projections about performance; 40% opportunity (lead) to appointment rate means we need 418 opportunities (leads) in total. Assuming an average of 1% Response Rate on Direct Mail, then we need 41,800 mail pieces for the year.

This is what the 50% of clients from direct mail strategy looks like in summary;

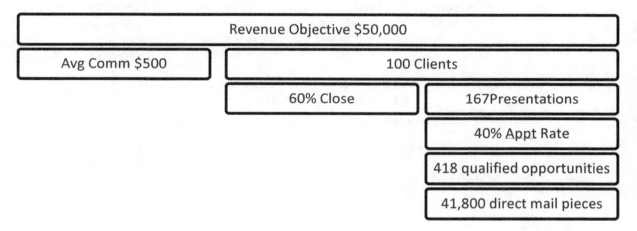

Revenue Objective $50,000		
Avg Comm $500	100 Clients	
	60% Close	167Presentations
		40% Appt Rate
		418 qualified opportunities
		41,800 direct mail pieces

This is where the tactics begin;

- Selecting the mail house(s)
- Determining the target demographic filters for desired product focus
- Testing direct mail creative for best response rate
- Measuring, monitoring and managing campaigns
- Meticulous follow up on leads received
- Selling and servicing clients for referrals and repeat business

What separates an agent from a Senior Insurance Advisor is planning. As it relates to your objectives, "Failing to plan is planning to fail".

Putting It All Together

Now you will build a strategic and tactical approach to generate 100k or more in 12-18 months. Because of the endless iterations and possibilities, this manual will provide real world guidance, but then day to day activities and financial goals **belong to you**. The worksheets are designed to be templates of the most common activities and should provide a good foundation of the tactics required to reach the objectives.

A reminder of the possibilities for 1st and 2nd year Senior Insurance Advisors;

Senior Insurance Advisor Portfolio Approach				
	Final Expense Foundation Product	**Medicare Supplement** (20% Of Clients Purchase)	**Medicare Advantage** (30% Of Clients Purchase)	**Hospital Indemnity** (30% Of Clients Purchase)
Total Clients	150	30	45	45

Revenue Opportunity					
	Final Expense	Medicare Supplement	Medicare Advantage	Indemnity	Total
Year 1	$57,600	$10,920	$12,765	$11,880	$93,165
Year 2	New $57,600 Renewal $4,500	New $10,920 Renewal $10,920	New $12,765 Renewal $9,585	New $11,880 Renewal $1,710	$119,880

Using this as your outline, by the 18th month, you should be just over 100k in annual income and have a stable, scalable and sustainable business as a Senior Insurance Advisor.

The breakdown of clients by product and by percentage were taken directly from the statistical experience outlined in Section 1, to provide a benchmark. Of course, your results will vary and you can build your own financial model based on product focus and commission opportunities.

Using the portfolio approach and all the information from the previous sections, the foundation product and driver of all core lead generation activity is Final Expense. That means you need;

150 Final Expense Clients

Everything else builds off of that activity, so our tactical focus will be predominatly on that audience until we have built a client base to warrant more balanced activities. If you already have a base of clients, then cater this Action Plan accordingly.

Where will these 150 clients come from?

A mix of all the lead generation activities outlined in the Securing Clients Section;

Canvassing – Telemarketing – Door Hanging – Mailers –

Presets – Direct Mail –

Repeat Business – Referrals

The tactics you engage will be determined by your resources of money and time, but until you have a prospective client to see…***you must be prospecting!!!***

Let's apply the same strategic approach we did in the previous example using this revenue matrix as our objective, with an understanding that the 150 Final Expense clients are the aim…the other elements will be a natural extension of those activities.

Client Distribution Projections

150 Final Expense Clients Distribution Projections		
20% Effort Based Marketing	40% Money Based Marketing	40% Skill Based Marketing
30 Clients	60 Clients	60 Clients
Canvassing Telemarketing Door-Hanging Mailers	Pre-Sets Direct Mail	Referrals for Final Expense

Next, we have to build sales projections so that we can fund our Money Based Marketing efforts while sustaining your household requirements. We will build a cash-flow model that is mindful of the fact you are "bootstrapping" your business from a lead generation perspective. The first months will be built on Effort Based Marketing and Referrals, and then begin to integrate Money Based Marketing efforts. There will be a natural scaling down of Final Expense activity as you prepare for the Annual Election Period (AEP), but of course, sales should be secured whenever the opportunity presents themselves!

Final Expense Sales Projections by Month by Source				
	Effort Based Marketing	Money Based Marketing	Referrals	Total
Jan	5	-	2	7
Feb	10	-	4	14
Mar	10	5	6	21
Apr	5	10	8	23
May	As needed	10	8	18
Jun	As needed	10	8	18
Jul	As needed	10	8	18
Aug	As needed	10	8	18
Sep	As needed	5	8	13
Oct	As needed	AEP Focus	AEP Focus	0
Not	As needed	AEP Focus	AEP Focus	0
Dec	As needed	AEP Focus	AEP Focus	0
Total	30	60	60	150

That will drive our cash flow;

Final Expense Cash Flow Analysis by Month		
	Sales	Gross Revenue
Jan	7	$2,688
Feb	14	$5,376
Mar	21	$8,064
Apr	23	$8,832
May	18	$6,912
Jun	18	$6,912
Jul	18	$6,912
Aug	18	$6,912
Sep	13	$4,992
Oct	0	$0
Not	0	$0
Dec	0	$0
Total	150	$57,600

Every industry has its natural peaks and cycles. We need to have some expectation of how revenue will come in throughout the year. This revenue will be used to fund all the activities of the business.

This analysis focuses only on Final Expense as the "base salary", understanding that the other products will happen throughout the year adding to the total revenue opportunity.

Depending on your product focus, current client base, and personal household needs, along with other factors, your model will be different.

Now we have a base of revenue to fund the Money Based Marketing Efforts. For this projection, that activity can be funded beginning March (3rd month of annual campaign) and 60 sales are projected from this channel. Since it is the only lead generation method that requires financing, we have to look at the potential costs and set targets for the campaigns.

60 Money Based Marketing Clients Needed

50% Direct Mail 30 Clients

50% Pre-Sets 30 Clients

From a similar approach using our Target and Tactics example, we need to assume a distribution percentage for Direct Mail and Pre-sets...a 50/50 mix is a good start and measuring, monitoring and managing campaigns will determine a different mix based on performance.

Direct Mail Campaign	
Metrics	Measurement
Costs	$4,000
# of Pieces	10,000
Response Rate	1.1%
# of Opportunities (BRC's)	110
Appt Rate	64%
# of Appts	70
Closing Rate	43%
# of Sales	30

Pre-Set Campaign	
Metrics	Measurement
Costs	$3,300
# of Appointments	110
Appt Rate	64%
# of Appts	70
Closing Rate	43%
# of Sales	30

These are the performance projections for the Money Based Marketing activities of Direct Mail and Pre-Set appointments. In this example, the total costs of both annual campaigns is $7,300 and will generate the objective of 60 sales.

Now all that is left to do, is to fund them based on the March – September cash flow expectations, do the work and measure, monitor and manage the results!

The professional Senior Insurance Advisor is doing more than selling a portfolio of products to a deserving senior population...they are running a business!

No business executes on a strategy without proper planning of revenue projections, marketing costs and tactical detail.

The time and energy spent engaging the activity of planning will protect your business, preserve your opportunity and allow you to reach the next level of your business.

Do it and expect the results!

Planning for Six-Figures

Now it is your turn to use the same approaches from the first part of this section to build your 12-18 month Action Plan. Be creative, understanding that there is no right or wrong answer...*only the answer that works for your business.*

Annual Revenue Worksheet

Senior Insurance Advisor Portfolio Approach				
	Final Expense Foundation Product	**Medicare Supplement**	**Medicare Advantage**	**Hospital Indemnity**
Total Clients				
Revenue Opportunity				
	Final Expense	Medicare Supplement	Medicare Advantage	Indemnity	Total
Year 1					
Year 2	New	New	New	New	
	Renewal	Renewal	Renewal	Renewal	

Final Expense Client Target: _____

150 Final Expense Clients Distribution Projections		
20% Effort Based Marketing	40% Money Based Marketing	40% Skill Based Marketing
30 Clients	60 Clients	60 Clients
Canvassing Telemarketing Door-Hanging Mailers	Pre-Sets Direct Mail	Referrals for Final Expense

Final Expense Sales Projections by Month by Source			
	Effort Based Marketing	Money Based Marketing	Referrals	Total
Jan				
Feb				
Mar				
Apr				
May				
Jun				
Jul				
Aug				
Sep				
Oct				
Not				
Dec				
Total				

Final Expense Cash Flow Analysis by Month		
	Sales	Gross Revenue
Jan		$
Feb		$
Mar		$
Apr		$
May		$
Jun		$
Jul		$
Aug		$
Sep		$
Oct		$
Not		$
Dec		$
Total		$

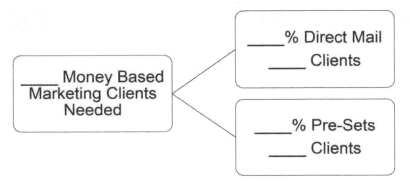

Direct Mail Campaign	
Metrics	Measurement
Costs	
# of Pieces	
Response Rate	
# of Opportunities (BRC's)	
Appt Rate	
# of Appts	
Closing Rate	
# of Sales	

Pre-Set Campaign	
Metrics	Measurement
Costs	
# of Appointments	
Appt Rate	
# of Appts	
Closing Rate	
# of Sales	

Go the extra step and break it down; tactics, activity and results, on a monthly basis. You are well on your way to 100k and beyond!

Monthly Portfolio Outlook				
	Final Expense Foundation Product	Medicare Supplement	Medicare Advantage	Hospital Indemnity
Total Clients				

This Months Revenue Opportunity				
Final Expense	Medicare Supplement	Medicare Advantage	Indemnity	Total

150 Final Expense Clients Distribution Projections		
20% Effort Based Marketing	40% Money Based Marketing	40% Skill Based Marketing
30 Clients	60 Clients	60 Clients
Canvassing Telemarketing Door-Hanging Mailers	Pre-Sets Direct Mail	Referrals for Final Expense

Final Expense Sales Projections by Month by Source and Revenue Generated				
Effort Based Marketing	Money Based Marketing	Referrals	Total Sales	Revenue Generated

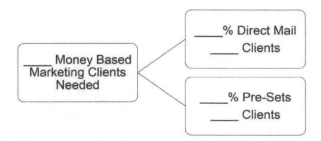

_____ Money Based Marketing Clients Needed

_____ % Direct Mail _____ Clients

_____ % Pre-Sets _____ Clients

Direct Mail Campaign	
Metrics	Measurement
Costs	
# of Pieces	
Response Rate	
# of Opportunities (BRC's)	
Appt Rate	
# of Appts	
Closing Rate	
# of Sales	

Pre-Set Campaign	
Metrics	Measurement
Costs	
# of Appointments	
Appt Rate	
# of Appts	
Closing Rate	
# of Sales	

Monthly Portfolio Outlook				
	Final Expense Foundation Product	**Medicare** **Supplement**	**Medicare** **Advantage**	**Hospital** **Indemnity**
Total Clients				
This Months Revenue Opportunity				
	Final Expense	Medicare Supplement	Medicare Advantage	Indemnity	Total

150 Final Expense Clients Distribution Projections		
20% Effort Based Marketing	40% Money Based Marketing	40% Skill Based Marketing
30 Clients	60 Clients	60 Clients
Canvassing Telemarketing Door-Hanging Mailers	Pre-Sets Direct Mail	Referrals for Final Expense

Final Expense Sales Projections by Month by Source and Revenue Generated				
Effort Based Marketing	Money Based Marketing	Referrals	Total Sales	Revenue Generated

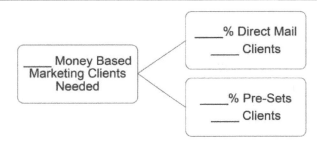

Direct Mail Campaign	
Metrics	Measurement
Costs	
# of Pieces	
Response Rate	
# of Opportunities (BRC's)	
Appt Rate	
# of Appts	
Closing Rate	
# of Sales	

Pre-Set Campaign	
Metrics	Measurement
Costs	
# of Appointments	
Appt Rate	
# of Appts	
Closing Rate	
# of Sales	

Monthly Portfolio Outlook				
	Final Expense Foundation Product	**Medicare Supplement**	**Medicare Advantage**	**Hospital Indemnity**
Total Clients				

This Months Revenue Opportunity					
	Final Expense	Medicare Supplement	Medicare Advantage	Indemnity	Total

150 Final Expense Clients Distribution Projections		
20% Effort Based Marketing	40% Money Based Marketing	40% Skill Based Marketing
30 Clients	60 Clients	60 Clients
Canvassing Telemarketing Door-Hanging Mailers	Pre-Sets Direct Mail	Referrals for Final Expense

Final Expense Sales Projections by Month by Source and Revenue Generated				
Effort Based Marketing	Money Based Marketing	Referrals	Total Sales	Revenue Generated

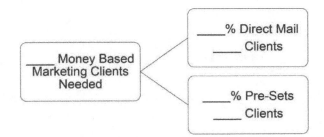

____ Money Based Marketing Clients Needed

____% Direct Mail ____ Clients

____% Pre-Sets ____ Clients

Direct Mail Campaign	
Metrics	Measurement
Costs	
# of Pieces	
Response Rate	
# of Opportunities (BRC's)	
Appt Rate	
# of Appts	
Closing Rate	
# of Sales	

Pre-Set Campaign	
Metrics	Measurement
Costs	
# of Appointments	
Appt Rate	
# of Appts	
Closing Rate	
# of Sales	

Monthly Portfolio Outlook				
	Final Expense Foundation Product	**Medicare Supplement**	**Medicare Advantage**	**Hospital Indemnity**
Total Clients				
This Months Revenue Opportunity				
	Final Expense	Medicare Supplement	Medicare Advantage	Indemnity	Total

150 Final Expense Clients Distribution Projections		
20% Effort Based Marketing	40% Money Based Marketing	40% Skill Based Marketing
30 Clients	60 Clients	60 Clients
Canvassing Telemarketing Door-Hanging Mailers	Pre-Sets Direct Mail	Referrals for Final Expense

Final Expense Sales Projections by Month by Source and Revenue Generated				
Effort Based Marketing	Money Based Marketing	Referrals	Total Sales	Revenue Generated

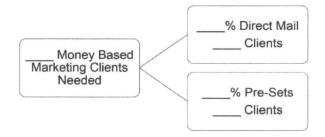

Direct Mail Campaign	
Metrics	Measurement
Costs	
# of Pieces	
Response Rate	
# of Opportunities (BRC's)	
Appt Rate	
# of Appts	
Closing Rate	
# of Sales	

Pre-Set Campaign	
Metrics	Measurement
Costs	
# of Appointments	
Appt Rate	
# of Appts	
Closing Rate	
# of Sales	

Month 5

Monthly Portfolio Outlook				
	Final Expense Foundation Product	Medicare Supplement	Medicare Advantage	Hospital Indemnity
Total Clients				

This Months Revenue Opportunity					
	Final Expense	Medicare Supplement	Medicare Advantage	Indemnity	Total

150 Final Expense Clients Distribution Projections		
20% Effort Based Marketing	40% Money Based Marketing	40% Skill Based Marketing
30 Clients	60 Clients	60 Clients
Canvassing Telemarketing Door-Hanging Mailers	Pre-Sets Direct Mail	Referrals for Final Expense

Final Expense Sales Projections by Month by Source and Revenue Generated				
Effort Based Marketing	Money Based Marketing	Referrals	Total Sales	Revenue Generated

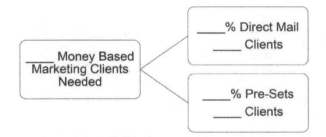

_____ Money Based Marketing Clients Needed

_____% Direct Mail _____ Clients

_____% Pre-Sets _____ Clients

Direct Mail Campaign	
Metrics	Measurement
Costs	
# of Pieces	
Response Rate	
# of Opportunities (BRC's)	
Appt Rate	
# of Appts	
Closing Rate	
# of Sales	

Pre-Set Campaign	
Metrics	Measurement
Costs	
# of Appointments	
Appt Rate	
# of Appts	
Closing Rate	
# of Sales	

Monthly Portfolio Outlook				
	Final Expense Foundation Product	**Medicare** **Supplement**	**Medicare** **Advantage**	**Hospital** **Indemnity**
Total Clients				

This Months Revenue Opportunity				
	Final Expense	Medicare Supplement	Medicare Advantage	Indemnity	Total

150 Final Expense Clients Distribution Projections		
20% Effort Based Marketing	40% Money Based Marketing	40% Skill Based Marketing
30 Clients	60 Clients	60 Clients
Canvassing Telemarketing Door-Hanging Mailers	Pre-Sets Direct Mail	Referrals for Final Expense

Final Expense Sales Projections by Month by Source and Revenue Generated				
Effort Based Marketing	Money Based Marketing	Referrals	Total Sales	Revenue Generated

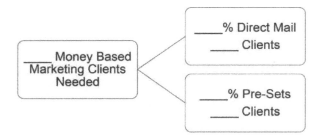

Direct Mail Campaign	
Metrics	Measurement
Costs	
# of Pieces	
Response Rate	
# of Opportunities (BRC's)	
Appt Rate	
# of Appts	
Closing Rate	
# of Sales	

Pre-Set Campaign	
Metrics	Measurement
Costs	
# of Appointments	
Appt Rate	
# of Appts	
Closing Rate	
# of Sales	

Month 7

	Final Expense Foundation Product	Medicare Supplement	Medicare Advantage	Hospital Indemnity
Monthly Portfolio Outlook				
Total Clients				

This Months Revenue Opportunity				
Final Expense	Medicare Supplement	Medicare Advantage	Indemnity	Total

150 Final Expense Clients Distribution Projections		
20% Effort Based Marketing	40% Money Based Marketing	40% Skill Based Marketing
30 Clients	60 Clients	60 Clients
Canvassing Telemarketing Door-Hanging Mailers	Pre-Sets Direct Mail	Referrals for Final Expense

Final Expense Sales Projections by Month by Source and Revenue Generated				
Effort Based Marketing	Money Based Marketing	Referrals	Total Sales	Revenue Generated

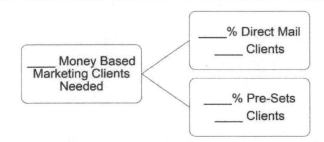

_____ Money Based Marketing Clients Needed

_____% Direct Mail _____ Clients

_____% Pre-Sets _____ Clients

Direct Mail Campaign	
Metrics	Measurement
Costs	
# of Pieces	
Response Rate	
# of Opportunities (BRC's)	
Appt Rate	
# of Appts	
Closing Rate	
# of Sales	

Pre-Set Campaign	
Metrics	Measurement
Costs	
# of Appointments	
Appt Rate	
# of Appts	
Closing Rate	
# of Sales	

Monthly Portfolio Outlook				
	Final Expense Foundation Product	**Medicare** **Supplement**	**Medicare** **Advantage**	**Hospital** **Indemnity**
Total Clients				

This Months Revenue Opportunity					
	Final Expense	Medicare Supplement	Medicare Advantage	Indemnity	Total

150 Final Expense Clients Distribution Projections		
20% Effort Based Marketing	40% Money Based Marketing	40% Skill Based Marketing
30 Clients	60 Clients	60 Clients
Canvassing Telemarketing Door-Hanging Mailers	Pre-Sets Direct Mail	Referrals for Final Expense

Final Expense Sales Projections by Month by Source and Revenue Generated				
Effort Based Marketing	Money Based Marketing	Referrals	Total Sales	Revenue Generated

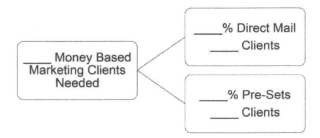

Direct Mail Campaign	
Metrics	Measurement
Costs	
# of Pieces	
Response Rate	
# of Opportunities (BRC's)	
Appt Rate	
# of Appts	
Closing Rate	
# of Sales	

Pre-Set Campaign	
Metrics	Measurement
Costs	
# of Appointments	
Appt Rate	
# of Appts	
Closing Rate	
# of Sales	

Month 9

Monthly Portfolio Outlook				
	Final Expense Foundation Product	**Medicare Supplement**	**Medicare Advantage**	**Hospital Indemnity**
Total Clients				
This Months Revenue Opportunity				
	Final Expense	**Medicare Supplement**	**Medicare Advantage**	**Indemnity**	**Total**

150 Final Expense Clients Distribution Projections		
20% Effort Based Marketing	40% Money Based Marketing	40% Skill Based Marketing
30 Clients	60 Clients	60 Clients
Canvassing Telemarketing Door-Hanging Mailers	Pre-Sets Direct Mail	Referrals for Final Expense

Final Expense Sales Projections by Month by Source and Revenue Generated				
Effort Based Marketing	Money Based Marketing	Referrals	Total Sales	Revenue Generated

_____ Money Based Marketing Clients Needed

_____% Direct Mail _____ Clients

_____% Pre-Sets _____ Clients

Direct Mail Campaign	
Metrics	Measurement
Costs	
# of Pieces	
Response Rate	
# of Opportunities (BRC's)	
Appt Rate	
# of Appts	
Closing Rate	
# of Sales	

Pre-Set Campaign	
Metrics	Measurement
Costs	
# of Appointments	
Appt Rate	
# of Appts	
Closing Rate	
# of Sales	

Monthly Portfolio Outlook				
	Final Expense Foundation Product	Medicare Supplement	Medicare Advantage	Hospital Indemnity
Total Clients				
This Months Revenue Opportunity				
	Final Expense	Medicare Supplement	Medicare Advantage	Indemnity	Total

150 Final Expense Clients Distribution Projections		
20% Effort Based Marketing	40% Money Based Marketing	40% Skill Based Marketing
30 Clients	60 Clients	60 Clients
Canvassing Telemarketing Door-Hanging Mailers	Pre-Sets Direct Mail	Referrals for Final Expense

Final Expense Sales Projections by Month by Source and Revenue Generated				
Effort Based Marketing	Money Based Marketing	Referrals	Total Sales	Revenue Generated

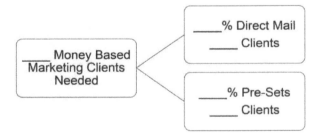

Direct Mail Campaign	
Metrics	Measurement
Costs	
# of Pieces	
Response Rate	
# of Opportunities (BRC's)	
Appt Rate	
# of Appts	
Closing Rate	
# of Sales	

Pre-Set Campaign	
Metrics	Measurement
Costs	
# of Appointments	
Appt Rate	
# of Appts	
Closing Rate	
# of Sales	

Month 11

Monthly Portfolio Outlook				
	Final Expense Foundation Product	Medicare Supplement	Medicare Advantage	Hospital Indemnity
Total Clients				
This Months Revenue Opportunity				
	Final Expense	Medicare Supplement	Medicare Advantage	Indemnity	Total

150 Final Expense Clients Distribution Projections		
20% Effort Based Marketing	40% Money Based Marketing	40% Skill Based Marketing
30 Clients	60 Clients	60 Clients
Canvassing Telemarketing Door-Hanging Mailers	Pre-Sets Direct Mail	Referrals for Final Expense

Final Expense Sales Projections by Month by Source and Revenue Generated				
Effort Based Marketing	Money Based Marketing	Referrals	Total Sales	Revenue Generated

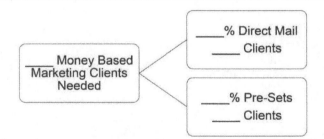

_____ Money Based Marketing Clients Needed

_____% Direct Mail _____ Clients

_____% Pre-Sets _____ Clients

Direct Mail Campaign	
Metrics	Measurement
Costs	
# of Pieces	
Response Rate	
# of Opportunities (BRC's)	
Appt Rate	
# of Appts	
Closing Rate	
# of Sales	

Pre-Set Campaign	
Metrics	Measurement
Costs	
# of Appointments	
Appt Rate	
# of Appts	
Closing Rate	
# of Sales	

Monthly Portfolio Outlook				
	Final Expense Foundation Product	**Medicare Supplement**	**Medicare Advantage**	**Hospital Indemnity**
Total Clients				
This Months Revenue Opportunity				
	Final Expense	Medicare Supplement	Medicare Advantage	Indemnity	Total

150 Final Expense Clients Distribution Projections		
20% Effort Based Marketing	40% Money Based Marketing	40% Skill Based Marketing
30 Clients	60 Clients	60 Clients
Canvassing Telemarketing Door-Hanging Mailers	Pre-Sets Direct Mail	Referrals for Final Expense

Final Expense Sales Projections by Month by Source and Revenue Generated				
Effort Based Marketing	Money Based Marketing	Referrals	Total Sales	Revenue Generated

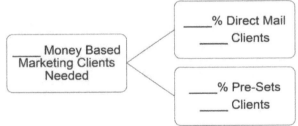

Direct Mail Campaign	
Metrics	Measurement
Costs	
# of Pieces	
Response Rate	
# of Opportunities (BRC's)	
Appt Rate	
# of Appts	
Closing Rate	
# of Sales	

Pre-Set Campaign	
Metrics	Measurement
Costs	
# of Appointments	
Appt Rate	
# of Appts	
Closing Rate	
# of Sales	

Section 6 Summary

Section Six Summary

- When it comes to your annual revenue goals, you can set whatever target you like but you must set an objective: *"If you don't know where you are going, you will probably end up somewhere else."* Lawrence J. Peter

- Strategy is your aim toward your target (Objective) and the tactics you use are your weapons…choose them wisely and use them effectively.

- Your Objectives, Strategies and Tactics must line up and all point to the same outcome.

- Layer your strategy until you have all the pieces of the puzzle in place…then prepare to execute the strategy with the corresponding tactics.

- The more detailed your planning, the greater chance for success as you can identify areas that may be off track in "real time" to make the necessary adjustments.

- Use Final Expense as the foundation product and build all projections from that as the primary marketing product.

- Build a cash flow analysis to project how revenue will come into your business throughout the year.

- Measure, Monitor and Manage all campaigns but particularly those that cost money to engage in.

- Plan your work and work your plan!

- Enjoy the reward of hard work and good service to your clients as a successful Six-Figure Senior Insurance Advisor!

End of Section Six

Congratulations on Completing <u>6 Hours to 6 Figures</u>!

If you have completed this entire <u>**6 Hours to 6 Figures**</u> Senior Insurance Advisor training manual, then I am confident you are well on your way to Six-Figures and helping 100's of people who are looking for someone to trust with some of their most critical insurance and healthcare decisions.

I know that the time we spent together is just the beginning of your journey. I am committed to your success and will continue to provide resources in support of this manual at

<u>www.brandonlclay.com</u>

Visit me often and sign up for updates to this program and live training events coming to your area!

Thank you again for giving me the awesome privilege of helping you on your road to great success...

I wish you Money, Power, Success!

B Clay

SECTION NOTES

SECTION NOTES

SECTION NOTES

Special Preview of Brandon's Books

Sales Crumbs from the Master's Table

Matthew Palmer was the sales "newbie" and LeRoy was the "old veteran". In an office where the young guns ruled with their smart phones, personal assistants, and expensive suits, no one seemed to have time or desire to coach the newcomer. Until one day, out of desperation, Matt approached LeRoy to show him the ropes. LeRoy responds to Matt by offering an intriguing proposition - pay for lunch everyday...*for a month.*

The resulting friendship, sales/life lessons, and Matt's ultimate success are an inspiring story of how the simplest things can bring the best results.

This is the must read volume that started it all!

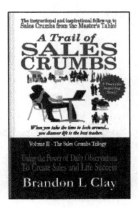

A Trail of Sales Crumbs

In this follow-up to <u>Sales Crumbs from the Master's Table,</u> we find Matt who has just finished 30 days of mentorship with LeRoy. A newly enlightened Matt begins to walk out the first steps of his journey - *still unsure of the future.* Revelation comes from his grandfather, *"It is not the big things that show you the way, but the little things...life is about the crumbs."*

Through a series of real world experiences, Matt discovers that the best answers come from unexpected places and that they guide you from struggle to the first signs of success.

This inspirational and instructional sequel continues the journey!

Feasting On Sales Crumbs

After creating a business roadmap with his colleagues, Matt finds himself immersed in a series of fast-paced interactions that lead him to the biggest sales opportunity of his life. Just when he thinks victory is imminent, he is faced with a difficult choice that may jeopardize the opportunity he has worked so hard for.

Using all the lessons he has learned, he listens to his heart and discovers that authenticity is the main ingredient for success and that daily joy is the beginning of "happily ever after".

This final volume is an information packed guide to sales and life success!

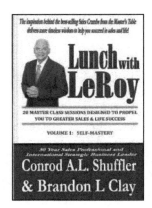

You met him in Crumbs...now enjoy

<u>Lunch with LeRoy</u> and continue the journey!

With over 50 years of sales distinction, Conrod Athelstan "LeRoy" Shuffler is internationally known as a sales philosopher and world-class trainer.

In <u>Lunch with LeRoy</u>, the principles, axioms and philosophies that have made him a living legend are now available to the newcomer as well as the seasoned professional. The knowledge in this First Volume is based on a lifetime of experience responsible not only his success but the success of 1,000's of others in the sales profession.

These 20 Sessions Will Change Your Professional and Personal Life!

Take a few moments to examine your life.

Is this where you thought you'd be **5 years ago?**
If you don't change now, where will you be in **5 more?**
Think it's too late?
It's never too late...
All that you desire is ***still possible***...

If You. Change. Now!

This program will work for you...regardless of where you find yourself today. It is progressive and uses proven techniques of success and achievement.

Coming July 2014!

Discovering and Unleashing Your

Authentic Sales Voice

All titles available on Amazon and at

www.brandonlclay.com!